All Color World of
SHIPS

All Color World of
SHIPS

Jonathan Rutland

F170

octopus

Contents

Jacket: A view of the retired P & O luxury
liner 'Queen Mary' at Long Beach,
California.
Endpapers: The steel barque 'Sindia' on the
Calcutta run.
Title page: Two frigates of the Royal Navy
'HMS Antelope' and 'HMS Amazon'.
This page: The sail training ship 'Royalist'.

First published 1978 by Octopus Books Limited
59 Grosvenor Street, London W1

Produced by Mandarin Publishers Limited
22a Westlands Road, Quarry Bay, Hong Kong

Printed in Hong Kong

From the earliest times to the Middle Ages

The story of ships begins in the unrecorded mists of prehistory. We can imagine early man observing tree trunks and branches floating in water, and finding out, perhaps as the result of accidentally falling into water, that he could hold on to them until he regained the safety of dry land.

Eventually primitive man discovered that a hollow log was more buoyant and capacious than a solid one, and he learned to tie together sticks, logs or even reeds with hide thongs or plant stems to make a raft. He found too that he could make a useful craft from an inflated animal skin—a 'boat' which remained in use until recent times in Asia, and which has been reborn in more recent times as the inflatable dinghy.

The use of paddles, and later oars, would have arisen naturally from propelling craft with hands and feet. Sails were probably invented accidentally when someone made the connection between the feel of the wind on his body and the motion of his boat following the wind.

Around the world people in remote areas still depend on traditional craft which differ little from the earliest rafts and dugouts. Papyrus boats on Lake Chad in Africa provide an example of this, but similar craft are found on Lake Titicaca in South America, and are known to have existed as early as 3000 BC on

Left: A traditional Arab dhow off the Mediterranean island of Djerba.
Below: Papyrus boats on Lake Chad in Africa.

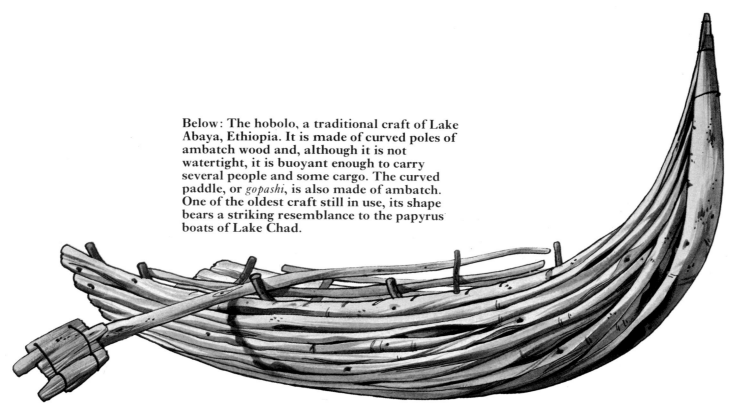

Below: The hobolo, a traditional craft of Lake Abaya, Ethiopia. It is made of curved poles of ambatch wood and, although it is not watertight, it is buoyant enough to carry several people and some cargo. The curved paddle, or *gopashi*, is also made of ambatch. One of the oldest craft still in use, its shape bears a striking resemblance to the papyrus boats of Lake Chad.

the Nile in Egypt. Constructed of bundles of reeds lashed together, and fitted with a bipod mast (i.e. one consisting of two verticals tied together at the top) and a single square sail made of papyrus slats or woven matting, they are very effective on calm inland waters. The reeds become waterlogged after a few months but with a plentiful supply of raw materials it takes little time or effort to build a replacement.

In coastal waters off Brazil and Taiwan rafts made of long logs or bamboo poles are used for fishing and for transportation. Unlike boats, these craft are not watertight—and for good reason. They ride safely through heavy surf which would quickly overwhelm a conventional boat. Both types have a single fore and aft sail, and when under way the crew lower keel boards between the raft's poles. These, like the centre board of a modern dinghy, help prevent the raft from being blown sideways by the wind.

In regions of Africa, Indonesia and other parts of the world, dugout canoes are still popular but they suffer from two main disadvantages. First, their long thin shape is unstable, a fault which is usually remedied by adding one or two outriggers, or by building double-hulled craft. Second, because a dugout is made by literally digging or hollowing out a tree trunk, its size depends on the trees available. In addition, a dugout beyond a certain length has little longitudinal strength. Its 'back' is easily broken.

Because the dugout is fashioned from a solid lump of timber, it was in that sense a dead end. However, although rather narrow in the beam, its smooth and streamlined shape slips through the water easily, and in this sense it pointed the way to the future. The raft is capable of oceanic voyages, as demonstrated by Thor Heyerdahl's *Kon Tiki*, but it proved to be a dead end

in another way. It is slow and awkward to manoeuvre. On the other hand it is a built up vessel. The development of the shipwright's art depended on combining the virtues of each type to create a vessel with ship-shape lines and a built up hull.

Ancient Egypt
The earliest archaeological evidence of boats and seafaring comes from the Mediterranean—where around 7250 BC craft were carrying cargoes of the volcanic flint obsidian between mainland Greece and the island of Melos. Oars found buried in bogs in Sjaelland, Denmark, and Yorkshire, England, date from about the same period. But the earliest actual boat so far discovered was buried in sand near the Great Pyramid of Khufu in Egypt, and most of our knowledge of early boats and ships comes from ancient Egypt. The Khufu boat, now excavated and rebuilt in a special museum, was a Nile river boat of about 2515 BC.

Records describe expeditions launched by the pharaoh Snefru around 2900 BC to Byblos in Phoenicia, and by Queen Hatshepsut who in about 1500 BC sent a major trading expedition to the 'Land of Punt'. Her ships returned laden with gold, myrrh, ivory, ebony and other exotic goods, and fortunately for posterity the queen was so delighted with the success of the venture that she had an illustrated account of it engraved on the temple walls.

The 'Land of Punt' is thought to have been on the coast of modern Somalia, so although the vessels doubtless hugged the coastline they were clearly an advance on earlier river boats. The latter were equipped with a single mast stepped (i.e. placed upright in a socket) near the bow carrying a square sail. This was satisfactory enough for sailing up the Nile with the prevailing following wind. But with the mast in that position the sail would inevitably keep the bow following the wind, making altering course or sailing across the wind difficult or impossible.

On Queen Hatshepsut's ships, in contrast, the mast was stepped amidships, so the sail no longer pulled the bow round into the wind. The bas reliefs show a complex system of rigging, with ropes called sheets and braces to hold the sail at an angle to the wind, and brails for reducing sail in stormy conditions. Thus the ancient Egyptian mariners brought the square sail rig to a very advanced state, and the ships would have been able to make headway even with the wind blowing from the side.

In fact the rig was far in advance of the hull structure, which was dictated by Egypt's lack of tall

trees. This ruled out dugout construction, and gave no scope for the timber framed and planked hull which was probably invented in Crete around 2000 BC. Forced to rely on timber from stunted and twisted acacia trees, the shipwrights of ancient Egypt devised an unusual hull made of short brick-like blocks of acacia. These were jointed and pegged together, and built up to form a large, thick and watertight hull— but one with no frame and therefore very little strength. A ship at sea is subject to two main stresses: transverse forces which tend to push the sides in or open them out, and longitudinal stresses which cause hogging or sagging (bending of the craft's 'back' as it rides over the waves). To improve transverse strength, stout

Below: Indian river boats. Rigged like the Arab dhow, the photograph shows clearly the long spar which carries the triangular lateen sail.

ropes were bound around the hull. These helped prevent the structure from collapsing outwards. For longitudinal strength, the Egyptian shipwrights invented the truss, a thick cable anchored to the hull at bow and stern and stretched tightly over raised crutches along the length of the ship.

The Khufu boat is 43·4 m (142 ft) long. The Punt expedition ships were shorter (probably around 27 m, 90 ft), but deeper, broader in the beam, and generally sturdier, more roomy, and better suited to their role as coastal merchantmen. On account of their greater capacity they were perhaps the first craft to justify the title of ship as opposed to boat. However, for the invention that was to revolutionize shipbuilding we must turn to ancient Crete.

Round ships and long ships

Some 500 years before Queen Hatshepsut's expedition sailed to the 'Land of Punt', Minoans on the Mediterranean island of Crete had evolved a method of ship construction which enabled them to build larger,

faster and more seaworthy ships than the Egyptians. Starting with a long log as a backbone or keel, the Minoan shipwrights built up a row of ribs along either side. The keel was curved up at the bow to provide a stempost, and keel and ribs together formed a sturdy frame which was then clad with timber planks.

The basic design was later improved by jointing stem and sternposts onto a more or less straight keel, and by fixing longitudinal stiffeners—known as wales—to the frame for additional strength. This framed and planked construction became the standard practice around the world until the advent of metal ships in the mid 19th century.

The Cretans took over from the Egyptians the role of merchantmen of the Mediterranean, and were in turn superseded by the Phoenicians from Tyre and Sidon on the shores of the eastern Mediterranean. More confident and adventurous than their predecessors, the Phoenicians probably circumnavigated Africa around 600 BC, and they regularly sailed north to Britain to trade in tin.

They evolved two distinct types of vessel: a round ship for trade, and a long ship for war. The round ship, so called because of its tubby shape, was capacious but awkward to manoeuvre, and slow. Primarily a sailing ship, it carried oars for auxiliary power. The long ship, or galley, was sleek and fast, and although it carried a single square sail this was always lowered before action, when propulsion was provided by ranks of oarsmen. This distinction between rowed warship and sailing merchantman lasted for some 2000 years until the Battle of Lepanto in 1571. Only then, with the development of the galleon, did the sailing ship acquire the speed and manoeuvrability essential for a warship.

The usual war galley was a bireme, which had two banks of rowers. The Greeks and Romans developed these craft further, building biremes, triremes and quinquiremes some 45 m (150 ft) long. They were fully decked, giving the rowers more protection and the soldiers a larger fighting platform. In the trireme (which had three banks of oars) the rowers probably

Left: Phoenician war galleys. Before battle the sail was lowered. The craft are biremes, that is, they have two banks of oarsmen. One bank sat in the central hull while the other was positioned in side decks curving out at each side. The narrow upper deck was a fighting platform, but the galley's other weapon is hidden beneath the water. It is a pointed ram which curves down and forward from the bow, and was an integral part of the hull. The war galley was a seagoing version of the battering ram.

sat on two levels, with two ranks along each side on the upper level—their oars resting on outriggers—and one on the lower level. Their seats would in this case have been angled across the ship so that the rowers did not get in each others' way. Nobody is sure how the quinquiremes were laid out, but a ship with five banks of rowers one above the other would have been impossibly top heavy and unstable. Perhaps the rowers were staggered slantwise on two decks, or perhaps there were five men to each oar. In any event the ancient war galleys, or 'pentekonters', were fearsome weapons of war.

While the Phoenician longship had a narrow hull extended outwards to accommodate the second rank of oarsmen, their round merchant ships had a much fuller and, by our standards, more conventional framed and planked hull. They often carried an ornamental horse's head on the stem post, and the stern post curved up above the hull in the form of a fish tail. Steering, as on the Egyptian ships, was by means of two large steering oars near the stern, and propulsion was via a single square sail.

Over the following centuries these sturdy craft evolved into the grain ships of Roman times. With a length to beam ratio of about three to one compared to the war galley's eight to one, these merchantmen of ancient times had four large holds under a fully planked deck, and could transport 250 tonnes of cargo and 300 or more people. The stern post was carved to resemble a sacred goose, while at the bow was a more important innovation in the form of a little sail called an 'artemon'. This was set on an angled spar—the precursor of the bowsprit—and its main purpose was not so much to add power as to steady the bow and make the ship easier to steer. The single mast carried the usual square sail with above it one or two triangular topsails.

Even so, the Roman grain ships were still desperately slow and awkward to handle except in a steady following wind. Their top speed is thought to have been about five knots. St Paul's lengthy voyage to Rome is narrated in the Acts of the Apostles, and the Roman author Lucian mentions the arrival of a grain ship at Piraeus, Greece, after a 70 day voyage from Alexandria—a distance of only about 725 km (450 miles) as the crow flies.

Junk and dhow
Roman merchant ships sailed throughout the Mediterranean, and northwards to Britain, but there was also a busy traffic from the Red Sea eastwards across the Indian Ocean. There the Romans and their successors would have met the very different craft of the Arabs and Chinese.

The Chinese junk was created from a cross between dugout and raft, by joining two dugouts with a platform of planks and building a large box-like superstructure on top. The Yellow River junk, the most primitive type, was aptly nicknamed a 'floating packing crate'. But in its more developed form the junk was a very advanced craft. With solidly constructed internal walls or bulkheads dividing the 'crate' into holds, it was immensely strong. And with a watertight cavity extending down through the hull near the stern for a proper rudder, it was much easier to steer than the Mediterranean vessels with their crude steering oars. In addition the junk had a remarkably efficient fore and aft sail which could be raised or shortened much as a Venetian blind is raised or lowered.

In a following wind a square sail is ideal. The craft is literally blown along. But because of the water's resistance the speed is naturally less than that of the wind. To travel across the wind the sail is set at an angle. Here entirely different forces come into play and they are exactly the same forces as those which lift an aircraft off the ground. Wind flowing around the outer edge of the sail speeds up because it has further to travel. By one of science's paradoxes this increase in speed causes a reduction of pressure. Wind meeting the inner face of the sail is slowed down, producing an increase in pressure. The combination of low pressure ahead of the sail and high pressure behind drives the craft forward. Once the vessel is moving, its own speed effectively accelerates the flow of air over the sail. To take full advantage of the aerodynamic 'lift' effect, a fore and aft sail set along rather than across the ship is needed. A well designed fore and aft rigger can sail faster than the prevailing wind. And a fore and aft rigged ship such as a junk is far more manoeuvrable than a square rigger, and much less dependent on the direction from which the wind is blowing.

The traditional Arab craft, the dhow, had by Mediterranean standards a more conventional hull than the junk, but like the latter it was fore and aft rigged. The leading edge of the dhow's enormous triangular lateen sail was attached to a long thin spar which was slung from the masthead and continued down to the bow. With this rig the dhow, like the junk, could tack, or zigzag, into the wind, an impossible feat on a square rigged ship. The dhow's spar could also be swung into a horizontal position across the craft to take full advantage of a following wind—an important virtue in the Indian trade, for the winds blow eastwards across the Indian Ocean in summer and westwards in winter.

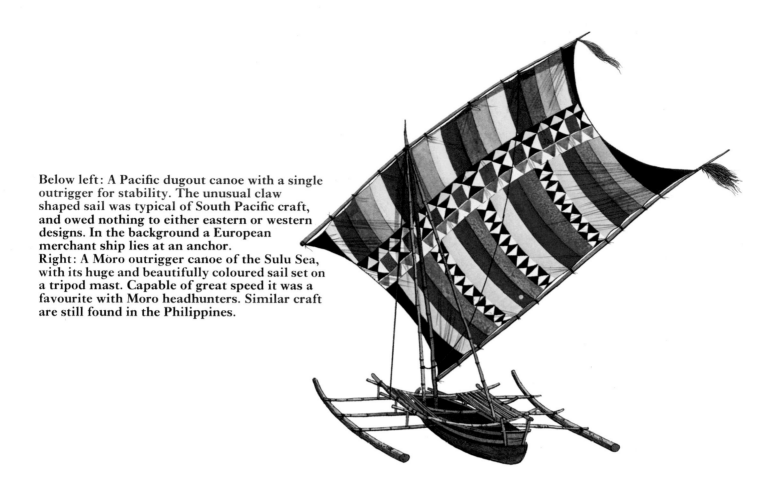

Below left: A Pacific dugout canoe with a single outrigger for stability. The unusual claw shaped sail was typical of South Pacific craft, and owed nothing to either eastern or western designs. In the background a European merchant ship lies at an anchor.
Right: A Moro outrigger canoe of the Sulu Sea, with its huge and beautifully coloured sail set on a tripod mast. Capable of great speed it was a favourite with Moro headhunters. Similar craft are still found in the Philippines.

The South Pacific

The traditional craft of the South Pacific peoples was and remains the dugout canoe. Built as a single hulled craft with outriggers, or with two hulls joined by connecting struts or a built up deck, it is a fishing boat, a means of transportation, a warship or a royal barge— as size and occasion demands. One type, the *lakatoi* of New Guinea, has three or more hulls and two masts carrying splendid claw-shaped sails. Some 18 m (60 ft) long and up to 15 m (50 ft) in the beam, the *lakatoi* is slow and clumsy, but buoyant, stable and well suited to long inshore voyaging.

At the other end of the scale are the light and fast Moro outrigger and the Hawaiian double canoe, a type found in the Pacific Islands and in New Zealand. Over 1000 years ago Maori inhabitants of Hawaii, Tahiti and Easter Island crossed and recrossed the Pacific Ocean in their large scale version of the double canoe, the *tainui*. These formidable craft were over 21 m (70 ft) long, with accommodation and storage space in the twin hulls and a large cabin for the chief and his followers on the deck joining them. The ornately decorated sternposts rose 6 m (20 ft) above the hull, and the *tainui* were propelled by twin claw shaped sails similar to those of the *lakatoi*.

The length of the Maori's migratory journeys between the Pacific Islands and to New Zealand is remarkable enough. The distance from Hawaii to New Zealand is well over 7000 km (4350 miles). But still more astounding is their ability to find their way there—and back again. Up to a point they could rely on the winds, which blow in a steady pattern across the Pacific. Their discovery of New Zealand must of course have been chance for they could not have known that it was there.

On their return they sailed north towards a star they called *Newe* in the southern hemisphere, heading for the Pole Star once they crossed the equator. The trick then was to know when they had reached the right latitude. According to tradition they solved this problem with a navigational instrument called the 'magic calabash'. It consisted of a gourd with its top cut off and five holes drilled in it—four of them on one level to ensure that when filled with water the instrument was held absolutely straight, and a fifth through which to sight the Pole Star. At any given latitude the Pole Star remains at a constant altitude (i.e. height above the horizon). The calabash would be 'calibrated' for the home island by drilling the fifth hole so that the Pole Star was visible through it. Thus on the homeward journey they simply sailed north until the calabash showed that they had reached the right latitude, and then turned east along that latitude.

The Vikings and Northern Europe

Early craft of northern waters include the familiar dugout, a particularly fine example of which was unearthed in Lincolnshire, England. This canoe, known as the Brigg boat, was 14·6 m (48 ft) long and 1·37 m (4·5 ft) wide—a remarkable size for a primitive stone age craft. Its makers devised an ingenious method of improving transverse strength by wedging crosspieces of timber inside the dugout and lashing thongs of rawhide across the hull to hold the sides firmly against the crossbeams. Another method used in ancient times to enlarge and strengthen dugouts was to soak them in a special solution containing animal fats and various salts. The craft could then be stretched and bracing struts inserted to strengthen it and hold it in shape.

Another boat favoured by northern mariners was the coracle or *currach*, a skin boat constructed from a frame of reeds or saplings covered with hides. The bullboats and *coritas* of American Indians were similar craft, as were the Eskimos' *uniaks*. Some skin boats were little more than one-man tubs suitable only for lake and river fishing. But others, including the *uniak* in which Eskimo seafarers hunted whales, and the Irish *currach*, were seagoing craft. Light, buoyant and fast, *currachs* carried Irish invaders to Britain and further afield. Irish legends describe a five year voyage in the 6th century by St Brendan the Navigator to

Below: The lavishly decorated prow of the Viking Oseberg longship. Excavated in a grave mound near Oslo, Norway, in 1903, this craft is smaller and less sturdily built than the Gokstad ship described in the text. The Oseberg ship was perhaps the pleasure craft of the woman whose remains and possessions were found buried on board.
Right: This 15th century picture of the Argonauts landing at Colchis shows the type of ship sailed by the Crusaders. It was basically a trading craft, the cog, with fighting 'castles' added at bow and stern.

Iceland and possibly even to North America.

This voyage may be a fanciful story, but with the exploits of the Vikings in their famed and notorious longships we are on surer ground. Their plundering forays to Britain were so common and fearsome that a new prayer was added to the litany: 'From the fury of the Danes, Good Lord, preserve us'. The Norwegians, almost as murderous as their Danish neighbours, sailed on raiding and trading expeditions to Britain, Ireland, northern France and into the Mediterranean. But they were avid explorers too, searching for new lands to settle.

The Norse sagas mention regular voyages to Iceland, and describe Erik the Red's discovery and colonisation of Greenland. Exploratory voyages were made westwards from there, and around the year 1000 Erik's son Leif Eriksson set sail with 30 fellows to investigate rumours brought back of unknown shores far to the west. After an arduous journey they reached a land where the foliage grew lush and green, the rivers and lakes abounded with salmon, and grapes flourished in the wild. Leif named the region Vinland —land of vines.

Attempts at colonisation failed, and the Vikings returned home. But they had in fact discovered the New World some 500 years ahead of Columbus. Vinland was probably on the coast of Newfoundland, although some think that the Vikings sailed further south, to Virginia or Maryland.

To confirm the possibility of such voyages an exact replica of the Gokstad ship, a Viking longship excavated in Norway in 1880, was sailed across the Atlantic. The original Gokstad ship, remarkably well preserved after 1000 years buried in blue clay, is now housed in a museum near Oslo, Norway, and provides a detailed record of Viking ship design and construction. The craft measures 23·8 m (76 ft) in length, with a beam of 5·1 m (17·5 ft) and a depth of 2 m (6·56 ft). Propulsion was via a single square sail, or by 32 oarsmen.

Unlike Mediterranean vessels, the Viking ships are double ended with pointed bow and stern, a feature that helped them ride safely in the rough northern waters. The hull is relatively broad in comparison to its length, and curves up at bow and stern; this very seaworthy design is still used today in lifeboats. And the planking is clinker built—that is, the planks overlap one another, giving greater strength (but less streamlining) than the flush carvel planking of Mediterranean craft.

A further notable feature of the Gokstad ship is that it has a true keel projecting down below the hull to give the craft a better hold in the water when sailing across the wind. Allied to this the Vikings evolved a system of bowlines to hold the square sail's leading edge taut, thereby improving performance in a side wind.

The Gokstad ship was probably a coastal craft, smaller and narrower than the ocean going vinland longships. The sagas describe huge warships known as *drekis* (dragons) 55 m (180 ft) long, with a complement of 700 men, while King Knut (Canute) was reputed to have launched a 91 m (300 ft) monster which carried 1000 warriors and 120 oarsmen.

Medieval ships

Little is known about the development of ships between the downfall of the Roman Empire and the Viking era towards the end of the first millennium AD. But by the end of this period the basic merchantmen of the Mediterranean had advanced dramatically beyond the cumbersome Roman grain ships. The hull had some of the grace and elegance of the Viking longship, with upward sweeping lines at bow and stern and a full beam amidships. However they were deeper in the water, and fully decked to accommodate the maximum amount of cargo. Their carvel built planking was nailed to the frame and caulked with pitch. And they retained the traditional pair of clumsy steering oars, in contrast to the Vikings' single oar. The latter was always on the right side of the ship, the 'steerboard'—or, as it came to be known in later terminology, 'starboard'—side.

But the most revolutionary feature of the 9th to 10th century Mediterranean ship was its lateen sail, which had been copied from the Arab dhow. The new ship design was strong, stable, seaworthy and easy to handle and steer in most wind conditions. With ever-increasing commerce in the Mediterranean and around Europe, shipwrights soon learned—like to-

day's tanker builders—to 'stretch' the ship, and larger and larger merchant vessels appeared. Two deckers were not uncommon by the middle of the 12th century, and three deckers followed some 100 years later. They were two masted, with three lateen sails on the main mast and two on the aftermast, which was shorter.

Mediterranean warships of the period also acquired two or three masts and lateen sails, and in contrast to earlier practice these were not lowered during battle. But the main driving force of the new war galleys, or dromonds (from the Greek *dromos*, a runner), was still provided by oarsmen. Two banks were now usual instead of the standard trireme of earlier times, with around 100 rowers in a 45 m (150 ft) long vessel. The bow ram had been moved above the waterline, and was accompanied by bronze tubes resembling fearsome demons from which the latest invention in the medieval arms race was pumped out by bellows. Known as 'Greek fire', it was a mixture of substances such as resin, oil, sulphur and phosphorus, and it wrought terrifying havoc and destruction. The dromond also carried a variety of *ballistae* which hurled javelins and other missiles at the enemy.

These formidable warships confronted the hastily converted merchant cogs of northern Europe in the sea battles of the Crusades. The cog, a broad and deep hulled craft, had evolved from the double ended longships of northern waters. Retaining the square rig and clinker planking of the longship, the cog was in most respects inferior to the larger, faster and more manoeuvrable ships of the Mediterranean. But for the western world it possessed a revolutionary new feature—a true stern rudder. The crusaders' warships were nothing more than cogs with fighting castles added at bow and stern.

By the 14th century guns had been added to the warships' armament. At first these were small hand held man killers, but by the time of the Battle of Lepanto ship killing broadside guns had made their appearance in the galleass. These ships, the ultimate in rowed warships, were so large that they needed the combined power of oar and sail. Their heavy firepower played a vital role at Lepanto. In this, the last great sea battle between rowed warships, some 200 Spanish and Italian galleys and galleasses defeated the Turkish pirate Ali Pasha's fleet of 273 galleys.

Below: A tangle of galleys in action at the Battle of Lepanto, 1571, by Micheli.

Carracks, galleons and men of war

With increasing trade between Northern Europe and the countries around the Mediterranean, meetings between the single masted square rigged northern cog and the three masted lateen rigged southern ship must have become commonplace. Shipwrights and mariners became familiar with both types, and during the 14th and 15th centuries they evolved a new vessel embodying the advantages of both.

Northerners adopted the flush carvel planking of the southern ships, thereby giving their vessels a smoother and faster passage through the water. Southerners in their turn copied the northerners' stern rudder. The overall hull shape became fairly standardized, with a rounded or squared off stern to accommodate the rudder, bluff 'apple cheek' bows to ride safely over rough seas, and a broad beam. The makeshift castles of the crusader ships became a permanent feature, with a single decked forecastle overhanging at the bow and a two or three tiered superstructure or 'aftercastle' at the stern usually consisting of half deck, quarter deck and poop.

Deep, broad, and in danger of becoming top heavy, these new carracks, as they were called, served as merchant ships and men of war. Piracy was an ever present danger, so both types carried guns in the superstructure.

The carrack's rig, like its hull, combined features of north and south, with a mixture of square and lateen sails. It was usually three masted, with at first two square sails on both fore and main mast, and a lateen on the after or mizzen mast. A small additional square sail reminiscent of the Roman 'artemon' but now named a spritsail was often rigged under a bowsprit. The original purpose of this spar projecting from the bow was to carry a stay which gave much needed extra support to the foremast.

Right: Carracks at the peak of their development as floating fortresses. The painting shows the English king Henry VIII embarking at Dover. With a length to beam ratio of around two to one, and with lofty castles fore and aft, carracks were splendid but unwieldy vessels. Despite the vast sail area they were slow, and success in battle resulted more from the brute strength of the men.

In time, as the carracks grew in size, the masts were lengthened by further spars which carried extra sails, and sometimes a fourth (lateen rigged) mast was stepped at the stern. The complex array of rigging required to support the masts and raise, lower and trim the sails looks like a sailor's nightmare, and descriptions of its development, function and terminology fill books. However, the basic arrangement was fairly straightforward. There were, and of course still are, two main types of rigging. One, the fixed 'standing rigging', supports the masts and consists of shrouds running from the mastheads to the ship's side for lateral support, and stays running between the masts and down to the bowsprit and the centre line of the hull for fore and aft support. The shrouds are criss-crossed by ratlines to provide rope ladders aloft. The other type, known as 'running rigging', can be subdivided into halyards, for raising and lowering yards and sails; sheets, which hold the foot of the sails down; braces, for setting and trimming the angle of the yards; and bowlines, for tautening the leading edge of a sail in a cross wind.

In view of the proven advantages of the lateen sail and the comparative simplicity of its rigging, it seems at first odd that the carrack's designers settled for a primarily square rigged ship. However, they had

Above: Spanish and English galleons in action at the Battle of the Armada, 1588, by Vroom. The large Spanish galleasses on the right played no significant part in this, the first major sea battle between sailing warships.

sound reasons for their choice. Above a certain size the lateen sail, with its long leading spar, becomes unmanageable. One can get a larger and more easily handled area of sail by positioning a number of square sails up each mast. Also, the fore and aft lateen sail's virtues are only significant if the ship has regularly to make headway in a cross wind. But, as was noted earlier, the winds in the Indian Ocean blow to a consistent pattern, and with correct timing a square rigger could be sure of a following wind on the outward voyage and on her return. When ships began crossing the Atlantic to the New World the prevailing winds again favoured the square rigger. In fact during Christopher Columbus' historic voyage in 1492 he altered the rig of one of his ships from lateen to square (his own ship, *Santa Maria*, was square rigged from the outset).

Above: English fireships heading for the Armada, whose close knit formation they effectively destroyed. Right: two details from Brueghel's 'Battle of the Gulf of Naples'. The towering castles of the 'floating fortress' ships can be clearly seen.

The development of the ocean going carrack occurred at a time when Europeans were looking for new horizons, from a spirit of adventure and discovery and for economic reasons. In 1453 the Moslems captured Constantinople, thereby completing their command of the eastern Mediterranean and of traditional trade routes to the east. This made it imperative for the Spaniards and Portuguese, who depended on revenues from commerce with the orient, to find new routes to the far east. The only hope appeared to be by sea, a factor which gave a vital stimulus to shipwrights and mariners alike.

Above: King Charles I of Britain's prestige man of war 'Sovereign of the Seas', by the contemporary artist John Payne. Launched in 1637, she was the largest and most advanced ship the world had seen—the prototype of the

British ships of the line that fought at Trafalgar in 1805.

There seemed to be two possibilities: to sail south down the west coast of Africa in the hope that there was a way round to the east, or to sail west around the globe to Asia. We must remember that nobody suspected the existence of America, because news of the Vikings' voyages had not been made widely known. So in theory the first landfall on sailing west should be in Asia. Estimates of the distance of the crossing ranged from 13,076 km (8,125 miles) or more by astronomers, to a mere 4,103 km (2,550 miles) by Columbus himself. As regards the African route, maps of the mid 15th century differed little from those drawn by Ptolemy in the 2nd century, and show Africa continuing endlessly southward.

The Spaniards concentrated their efforts on the westward route, which was eventually discovered by the combined efforts of Columbus, Vespucci and Magellan. Their vessel was the carrack. Columbus' ship *Santa Maria* was probably some 24·5 m (80 ft) in length and 8 m (26 ft) in the beam, with a lateen mizzen sail, two square sails on the main mast, one on the foremast, and a spritsail under the bowsprit. She probably looked much like a scaled down version of a carrack.

The Portuguese explorers Bartolomeo Diaz and Vasco da Gama sailed south seeking a way around Africa, and for this they had to have a ship capable of beating into the wind. Their ships were caravels, the successors of the 10th century Mediterranean lateen rigged merchantmen. With a shallower draught and more graceful lines than the carrack, the *caravela latina*—the type used by the Portuguese explorers—had two or three lateen rigged masts. The *caravela redonda*, however, had square sails, or a combination of square and lateen like the carrack.

The caravel normally had no forecastle and a comparatively small superstructure at the stern. The carrack, however, continued to grow in height, with ever more elaborate fore and aftercastles. These towering ships were top heavy enough at the best of times, and heavy cannon mounted in the superstructure only aggravated the problem. An invention of the early 1500s helped to alleviate the carrack's instability. This was the gunport, an opening cut in the hull itself. Now the massive bronze or brass guns could be moved down into the hull, bringing the ship's centre of gravity back to a more acceptable and seaworthy level. With a row of cannon along each 'broadside', stern chasers at the back, and an array of smaller guns which could be fired down from both fore and after castles, the early 15th century carrack fully earned its nicknames 'floating fortress' and 'great ship'.

Left: The 'Resolution', 1669, by William van de Velde the younger. She was a 70 gun third rate ship of the line.

The birth of the galleon

Carracks were, however, still dual purpose craft. They were merchantmen, bringing back—for example—Spanish treasure from the New World, and they were fighting ships. In the latter role, despite their impressive armament, they left a great deal to be desired. With their vast bulk and height above the water they were slow and awkward to handle. So although kings and ministers of state enjoyed the prestige of a fleet of great ships, the actual seafarers who had to man them were less content. They wanted a new type of vessel, a specialized sailing warship with the carrack's fire power and the galleass's manoeuvrability—hence the birth of the galleon.

The name galleon was Spanish in origin, and came from 'galley', which by the 16th century probably simply meant 'warship'. However, the galleon did inherit certain features from the later war galleys. It was significantly slimmer than the carrack, with a length to beam ratio of one to three, and it had the galley's characteristic beak, a long low structure projecting from the bow below the bowsprit. The carrack's overhanging triangular forecastle was replaced by a more modest square fronted structure at the foot of the foremast, and although the galleon retained the carrack's tiered arrangement of half deck, quarter deck and poop aft of the main mast, the aftercastle was altogether lower and more trimly faired into the body of the ship.

The English were the first to perfect the 'race built' galleon. Elizabethan galleons such as Drake's favourite ship the *Revenge*, and the *Ark Royal*, designed and built by Sir Walter Raleigh but bought from him by the state, were about 36·5 m (120 ft) long overall and displaced a mere 500 tonnes. The length on the gun deck—the first deck below the upper or main deck (i.e. the top deck of the hull proper)—would have been some 30·5 m (100 ft), and the beam about 9·75 m (32 ft). The heaviest guns, long range culverins, as they were called, were mounted on this gun deck, with 12 along each broadside. The after section was stepped down for the sternmost pair of guns on either side, allowing the stern superstructure to be lowered, and with it the galleon's centre of gravity. A further battery of rather smaller guns were carried on the upper deck.

Overall the race built galleon was sleeker than the carrack, and lower in the water, both factors improving its speed and general sailing qualities. It was armed with longer range guns. And it carried a total complement of some 250 men: 150 sailors, 30 gunners and 70 soldiers. It was designed for 'hit and run' fighting, where speed and flexibility were crucial—in the ship and in its crew. In action, sailors and soldiers doubled as gunners when required, and if it came to a hand to hand fight, gunners and sailors fought alongside the soldiers.

The Battle of the Armada

The English galleon fulfilled Raleigh's requirements:

> First, that she be strong. Secondly, that she be swift. Thirdly, that she be stout sided. Fourthly, that she carry her guns all weather. Fifthly, that she hull and try well, which we call a good ship. Sixthly, that she stay well, when bourding and turning on a wind is required.

The Spanish galleons which met the English in 1588 in the Battle of the Armada Raleigh dismissed:

> The great ships are least serviceable, go very deep to water, and are of marvellous charge and fearful cumber . . . They are less nimble, less maineable, and very seldom employed . . . A ship of 600 tons will carry as good ordnance as a ship of 1200 tons, and though the greater have double her number, the lesser will turn her broadsides twice before the greater can wend once.

The contemporary English geographer and writer Richard Hakluyt writes of the Spanish galleon's 'huge bignesse', and adds that they are 'so high that they resembled great castles, most fit to defend themselves and to withstand any assault'. The lower framing and planking he says was 'foure or five foote in thickness, insomuch that no bullets could pierce them'.

He was right about the last point. The English tactic was to fire heavy broadsides 'on the downward roll', in the hope of crippling the enemy ship by holing it below the waterline. This idea was a failure; the culverins had the range, but not the power. Fortunately for the English, the Spaniards found themselves unable to employ their favoured close combat tactic. This entailed firing on the upward roll to cripple the enemy by dismasting him, and then closing in, grappling and fighting a land style hand to hand battle. Their ships were indeed 'most fit to defend themselves', but they were unable to attack their nimbler foes effectively.

Thus, when on 31 July, 2 August and 4 August 1588 the 130 ships of the Spanish Armada met the English fleet of 197 ships, many of which were comparatively small, neither side was able to inflict any serious damage on the other. The action resembled that of an agile puppy barking viciously at the heels of an elderly alsatian. However the battle warmed up on 6 August, when the Armada anchored off Calais, France. The English, at dead of night, sent six fire-ships into the midst of the enemy fleet. These caused a certain amount of damage, but more importantly they created panic and confusion. The Spaniards cut their anchors and in the darkness their close formation

Above left: European frigates in action in the late 18th century.
Above: A French and a British brig in close combat. The brig was square rigged on both masts. In addition it carried a fore and aft 'brig' sail (later to be called a gaff) on the after mast, and a large jib set on a jib-boom (a spar extending from the bowsprit).

was irretrievably lost. This enabled the English to dart in and out amongst the disorganized Spanish fleet, wreaking considerable destruction. The remainder of the Armada fled, losing many more ships in storms as it worked its way around the British Isles and across the Atlantic back to Spain. Of the 130 ships that set out, only 67 returned home.

Quite apart from its political significance, the Battle of the Armada signalled the beginning of a new era in naval warfare. It was the first large scale battle between sailing warships, and the first in which 'modern' warships designed to kill from a distance were employed. The Spanish galleons and their forerunners were essentially troopships which engaged in land style close combat. The English galleons were the first true battleships.

Ships of the line—the broadside era
Our knowledge of early galleons comes from contemporary illustrations, writings and a few rough hewn models, and from interpretation of this often inadequate or suspect material by naval historians, artists and shipwrights. In 1973 a full-scale replica of *Golden Hind*, the galleon in which Drake circumnavigated the globe in the 16th century, was launched and sailed across the Atlantic. But much of the ship's detail, and indeed dimensions, were based on surmise.

With the successors to the Armada race built galleons—larger and more powerfully gunned vessels such as the English prestige ship *Sovereign of the Seas* and the Swedish *Wasa*—we have a much clearer and more comprehensive picture. This is in part because it became common practice to build detailed models, to give naval authorities something concrete on which to base their deliberations. But much more to the point, we have an actual ship to study: the *Wasa*.

Wasa was ordered by the Swedish king Gustavus Adolphus, built in Stockholm by a Dutch master shipwright, and launched in 1628. Her maiden voyage, accompanied by much pomp and ceremony, lasted only a few minutes. As she sailed across Stockholm harbour a squall of wind heeled her over. Water gushed rapidly in through the open gunports of the lower gun deck, and she sank, leaving nothing but the masthead showing above the water.

There followed a long and heated but inconclusive enquiry. The disaster may have been due to nothing more than bad luck and carelessness. Capsizing is an ever present danger with tall masted sailing ships, especially with the lower gunports open. Perhaps the ship was inadequately ballasted, or perhaps, as the sailing master alleged, *Wasa* had too much 'top hamper' (i.e. too much gear too high up for stability). At any event, despite numerous attempts at salvage *Wasa* remained buried in the mud of Stockholm harbour for over three centuries until she was rediscovered in 1956. The hull was finally raised in 1961.

A sumptuously decorated man of war designed to arouse the Swedish navy's fighting spirit and intimidate the enemy, *Wasa* measures 39 m (128 ft) on the keel and 11·68 m (38·33 ft) in the beam. Her overall length is a full 61 m (200 ft), and her displacement has been calculated at around 1300 tonnes. A three master with a ship's company of 437 men, she carried 64 guns—48 of them on two gun decks.

The English man of war *Sovereign of the Seas*, launched in 1637, was even larger, but she still retained the elegant and seaworthy lines of the race built galleon. As refashioned in the 1650s her overall length stood at 71·32 m (234 ft), her keel at 41·3 m (135·5 ft), her gun deck at 51·13 m (167·75 ft), and her beam was 14·63 m (48 ft). She mounted 100 guns on three flush decks and carried a much greater spread of sail than any earlier ship, with four square sails on both fore and main masts, two square and one lateen on the mizzen, and spritsails above and below the bowsprit. Her top speed was probably around 9 knots.

When the plans were drawn up, naval experts complained that *Sovereign of the Seas* would be too large and top heavy, and she did indeed prove to be a somewhat unwieldy ship to handle. She was also a little too narrow in relation to her length to provide a stable gun platform. However, she was the prototype of the British man of war until the end of the sailing warship era, and had she survived she would have made a welcome addition to the British fleet at the Battle of Trafalgar in 1805.

Wasa, *Sovereign of the Seas*, and other ships like them were ships of the line. This expression describes the basic tactic of sea warfare evolved in the 17th century which was to last until the early 19th century. The principal warships of the fleet sailed into battle in line ahead, thereupon unleashing their broadsides at the enemy, who entered the action and employed their broadsides similarly. This formalized routine differed radically from the hit and run methods used by the English at the Battle of the Armada, and success depended more on the power of the cannon and accuracy of the gunners than on the ships' agility. Battle was normally joined at close quarters, and although the earlier long range culverins retained a place, the ships were in the main armed with shorter range cannon firing much heavier shot. In the earlier Spanish tradition, the heavy gun battle was followed up by grappling, boarding, and hand to hand combat on deck.

The ships were classified into rates, determined at first by the number of men on board, and later by the number of guns. A first rater mounted 100 or more guns, a second rater between 80 and 100, a third rater between 50 to 80, while a fourth rater had from 40 to 50. The first to fourth raters were ships of the line, but the smaller rates did not join the battle line.

Developments in warship design and rig

During the late 17th and 18th centuries various improvements in detail were made to the basic design set by ships like *Wasa* and *Sovereign of the Seas*, and Britain's lead in warship construction passed to the Dutch and French. The hull shape lost the upward curving lines at bow and stern, thereby providing flatter decks, and it also lost the 'tumble home'—the inward slanting sides of the upper hull.

The hull and superstructure also lost most of the elaborate and costly decoration, gaining a more business like appearance, while below the waterline shipwrights at last found a way of sheathing the hull in copper. This prevented attacks by the destructive marine version of the familiar household woodworm, the teredo or ship worm. It also discouraged other marine plants and animals, thus giving ships smoother underwater lines and increased speed.

The primitive tiller had been succeeded by the whipstaff in the 16th century. This vertical lever ran up through the decks from the tiller, allowing the steersman at least a partial view of the sails and placing him in earshot of the captain. Early in the 18th century the whipstaff was at last replaced by the far more efficient wheel, which swung the rudder through a system of ropes and pulleys.

The basic square rig of the early ships of the line was retained, but overall efficiency and flexibility were transformed by the addition of more fore and aft sails, and by replacing the mizzen lateen sail with a gaff sail set on a long boom extending over the stern. This new sail was called a driver, or, on merchant ships, a spanker. Triangular fore and aft staysails were set on mainstay, main topmast stay, mizzen stay and fore topmast stay, and later a series of foresails called jibs appeared, set on a new spar, the jib-boom, which was simply an extension of the bowsprit.

Above right: The Battle of the Saintes, 12 April 1782, an encounter in which the British fleet commanded by Admiral Rodney decisively defeated the French, thereby averting the latter's threat to Jamaica.
Right: While the 'Battle of the Glorious First of June' 1795 (in the French Revolutionary War) rages in the background, Admiral Howe stands on board HMS 'Queen Charlotte'.

The end of the wooden warship era

By 1800 the most common ship of the line was the 74 gun third rater. Some first raters mounted 130 or more guns, but for most purposes the third rater was large and heavily armed enough, and its speed and manoeuvrability amply compensated for its lack of size. These features were especially important to the British Admiral Nelson who commanded the Royal Navy at the Battle of Trafalgar in 1805, for he boldly decided to throw away centuries of tradition by not sailing into action in line ahead.

Nelson had 27 ships of the line. Opposed to him was the allied fleet of France and Spain under Admiral Villeneuve, with 33 ships of the line. Villeneuve formed his fleet into the usual single file and Nelson, dividing his ships into two squadrons, attacked at right angles.

Left: The British fleet sailing in line ahead engage the French at the Battle of the Nile, 1798.
Below: The Battle of Copenhagen, 1801—an easy victory for Nelson.

The British ships broke through the allied line, shattering its formation in the process. In the ensuing mêlée, which was exactly what Nelson had planned, the superiority of the British sailors and the independence given to their commanders by Nelson's plan of action soon took their toll. At the end of the day Nelson himself was dead, killed by a sniper's bullet, but the British had won a decisive victory, capturing 22 enemy ships without themselves suffering a single loss. Trafalgar initiated a century of British supremacy at sea and ended the age of the set piece broadside battle.

Victory, Nelson's flagship at Trafalgar, carried 102 guns. The 30 14·5 kg (32 lb) cannon on the lower gun deck each needed a crew of 15 men. Their maximum range was nearly 2·5 km (1·5 miles), while at about 460 m (500 yd) their shot could penetrate 1 m (1·1 yd) of timber. *Victory* however was less remarkable for her armament or size than for her massive timbers. Her oak built double hull was

Above: The 'Royal George' off Deptford, by Clevely the Elder. Two men of war are also shown at different stages of construction. 'Royal George', a 100 gun first rater, sank at her moorings at Spithead, England, in 1782.

designed to withstand close fire from the heaviest guns of the time. She served as flagship in four major battles, and survives to this day standing in dry dock at Portsmouth, England.

Victory was not the only massively built ship at Trafalgar. The French and Spanish ships were generally considered superior to the British. It is interesting to note that in the entire battle not one ship of the line was sunk, although many were of course battered and dismasted, and thousands of men were killed.

Supporting the ships of the line in the later battles of the broadside era was a new generation of smaller warships. These included frigates, three masted vessels with around 36 guns on a single gun deck, for escort, patrol and raiding duties. There were also brig rigged sloops and corvettes, single masted cutters, and fore and aft rigged schooners—all acting as scouts, patrol boats or gunboats as different occasions demanded.

The American War of Independence stimulated ship development in the New World. American ship-wrights studied European warships and their own Baltimore clipper merchantmen before starting work on their own fleet. Their choice of vessel was the frigate. They could not hope to build enough capital

ships to match the British navy in a pitched battle. But they could and did create a small navy of fast frigates which were unequalled, and which inflicted damage and confusion on the British out of all proportion to their size or number.

The most famous, *Constitution*, was 62·18 m (204 ft) long overall, 13·26 m (43·5 ft) in the beam, and displaced 2200 tonnes. With 30 cannon on the gun deck, 22 carronades (short range wide bore guns aptly nicknamed 'smashers') on forecastle and quarter-deck, and a startling top speed of 13·5 knots, she fulfilled her designer's promise that her commander should have it in his power to engage any ship or not as he thought proper. *Constitution's* most notable victory was over the British frigate *Guerrière*. Affectionately known as 'Old Ironsides', she has been restored and is berthed in the Boston Navy Yard.

Life at sea

The seaman's lot on a man of war was nasty, brutish, and usually short. Before embarking on a long voyage the captain always took on a much larger crew than he needed to allow for the inevitable depredations caused by disease. Yet with a complement of nearly 450 men a ship such as the *Wasa* was crowded enough at the best of times.

Most of the crew lived and messed on the gun decks, sleeping in hammocks slung from the beams, and eating at tables between the massive guns. Here gratings in the upper deck let in light and air, and in fair weather the gunports could be opened. Less fortunate members of the ship's company lived on the orlop, the next deck down. This was below the water-line, so there was no natural light and little fresh air could circulate at this level.

Officers fared rather better, with individual cabins in the after part of the upper gun deck. But they too were sandwiched between guns, and their cabin walls consisted of movable canvas or wooden screens which had to be cleared away before action. 'A thing much like to some gentleman's dog kennel' was one officer's description. Above was the great cabin occupied by the captain, who lived in some style and comfort, and whose diet included the luxury of fresh meat provided by slaughtering animals kept in pens on the upper deck.

The ordinary seaman's diet was notably lacking in fresh food of any description. His daily ration might include up to 1·36 kg (3 lb) of bread and hard biscuit, around 0·45 kg (1 lb) of salt meat or fish, and 4·55 litres (1 gallon) of beer. This was supplemented by dried peas, butter and cheese. The fish and meat were

Above: The Battle of Trafalgar, 1805. The picture shows the confused mêlée after the British had broken the French line.

often too hard to eat, the beer sour, the butter and cheese rancid and the biscuits and peas so full of weevils that the men preferred to eat in the dark. The words of a midshipman of the mid 18th century describe the effects, and add a further touch of horror:

> The crew are extremely sickly, they having very few capable of working the ship; and what still adds to their unfortunate condition is the prodigious increase of rats, which plague them to that degree that they can get no sleep; for they are no sooner laid down in their hammocks, but immediately a swarm of these vermin come running over them and frequently give them sad bites.

The writer goes on to describe 'the destruction which these vermin make on the dead bodies that lie about the deck (they having at this time ten to a dozen dying in a day)'.

Until 1753, when the benefits of lemon juice were realized, scurvy (vitamin C deficiency) was the main killer, but on a voyage through tropical waters the crew were ravaged too by epidemics of infectious diseases. Sanitation was limited to an occasional

37

'sweetening' of the ship's interior by a thorough washing down with vinegar.

Discipline was harsh, with punishments ranging from hanging from the yardarm, keel hauling and flogging (the latter for even minor offences), to 'holding'. This was reserved for younger members of the crew who were shut up in the stench and isolation of the hold, with a lantern to encourage the rats and cockroaches.

The Duke of Wellington summed up the situation nicely when, after a voyage in a man of war, he said to the captain: 'Everything goes like clockwork, sir, but I would not command an army on the same terms as you do your ship—not for the crown of England. I have not seen a smiling face since I have been aboard'.

Above: The French frigate 'La Bayonnaise' and the English frigate 'Amuscade' in a ship to ship action on 14 December 1798, by Crépin.
Right: The famous duel between the American and British frigates 'Constitution' and 'Guerrière', 1812, by Birch.

East Indiamen and clippers

By the early 1800s myriad types of merchant ships had evolved, from small coastal yachts, fluyts and brigs through ocean going whaleships to the lord of them all, the East Indiamen. Portly craft with holds deep enough to stow 2400 barrels of oil, the square rigged three masted whalers were among the most unpopular of all ships. Voyages commonly lasted for

Above left: William H. Webb's medium clipper 'Challenge', 1853.
Below left: American and British whaleships and boats off the Cape of Good Hope early in the 19th century.
Below: One of the most famous of all clipper races, between 'Taeping' and 'Ariel', took place in 1866 when they sailed from Foochow, China, to London, England. After 99 days at sea, 'Taeping' won by just 20 minutes.

four years or more—the seamen's 'post box', a turtle shell on the Galapagos Islands, often held letters several years old; the dangers, from storms and leaky timbers to say nothing of the whales, were considerable; and the stench was foul (the blubber was boiled down on board). American whalers, based at Nantucket and New Bedford, dominated the industry, sailing the length and breadth of the Pacific Ocean. The destruction of the Nantucket whaleship *Essex* in 1829—she was rammed by a sperm whale—gave Herman Melville the setting for his novel *Moby Dick*.

Another *Essex*, this one a British East Indiaman, has the distinction of being a record breaker, setting the largest suit of sails of all time. Of the amazing total of 63, 21 were set on the mainmast, with—starting at the foot—course, topsail, topgallant, royal and skysail

(the usual five), followed by cloudscraper, moonraker and stargazer. At either side of the lower five, stun' sails (or studding sails) could be set, vastly increasing sail area and power in a following wind. In addition there were the by now normal spence, a gaff fore and aft sail at the foot of the mast, and staysails.

French, British and Dutch East Indiamen engaged in trade between Europe, India, the East Indies and China. Each company held a monopoly of trade to its own territories, so speed was of less consequence than capacity and endurance. Despite their impressive spread of sail they were slow ships, justly earning their later nickname as 'tea wagons'. The round trip to China and back usually lasted over 12 months.

Also called 'fat East Indiamen', they were both fat in the beam, and in the rewards they offered master and crew. Discipline, as in the navy, was strict, but conditions, food and prospects were good and there

was never any shortage of recruits.

With the ever present threat of pirates in eastern waters, and of hostile men of war and privateers, East Indiamen were well armed, mounting a normal complement of between 26 and 40 large cannon on the middle deck. To discourage attackers gunports were painted on at the lower deck level to give the ship the appearance of a full man of war. *Essex*, one of the first ships to be 'camouflaged', was painted differently on either side to confuse potential enemies.

From schooner to Baltimore clipper

Many of the smaller merchantmen were primarily square rigged. Collier brigs, cargo versions of the naval brigs pictured in the previous chapter, are one example. Brigantines and snows are others. The snow differed from the brig in setting a 'snowsail' instead of a brigsail at the stern. The sail was identical but

instead of being stepped on the mainmast, where the brigsails' rigging could foul that of the mainsail, it was set on a short mast just aft of the mainmast. The first brigantines differed from brigs only in the absence of the brig sail, while later brigantines were fore and aft rigged on the mainmast.

However, increasing numbers of fore and aft rigged merchantmen were evolved for work where speed and manoeuvrability were important. Descendants of the dhow and caravel, these included cutters, ketches and schooners. The cutter, a single master with a mainsail, two or more headsails, and in its earliest forms an additional square sail or two, was a favourite with smugglers—and with their opponents, the revenue men. Cutters also ran mail and pilot services, and later became popular for pleasure cruising and ocean racing.

The ketch, with in European waters its traditional

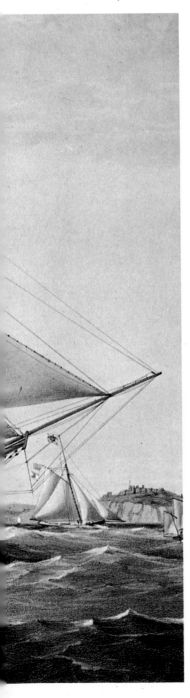

Left: 'Anglesey', 1852, a Blackwall frigate. These ships—so called because they were built at Blackwall on the Thames, England— were more heavily and solidly constructed than clippers, and lacked their very fine lines, especially at the bow. Sailing mainly on the India run, they were successors to the fat East Indiamen, and represented a compromise between the the 'tea wagons' and the true clippers.

tan coloured sails, was essentially a 'stretched' cutter with two masts, while the schooner was larger, slimmer and faster. Probably evolved by the Dutch in the 17th century, the schooner rig came in a confusing variety of forms. Its two or more masts normally carried fore and aft gaff sails, above which there might be square (or square and fore and aft) topsails (the topsail schooner), or just fore and aft topsails (the fore and aft schooner). Then again there were hermaphrodite schooners, square rigged on the foremast and with both square and fore and aft sails on the mainmast.

Taking the schooner rig, and the hull form of the Jamaica or Bermuda sloops which traded between the West Indies and the east coast of America during the 18th century, shipwrights of the Chesapeake Bay, New York and Massachusetts area created a remarkable new ship which became known as the Baltimore clipper. Steeply raked at bow and stern, with fine V-shaped underwater section and a hull reminiscent of the race built galleons in its graceful upward curving lines fore and aft (but with no superstructure at all), these Baltimore clipper schooners sliced through the water with less effort and far greater speed than the ttaditional 'apple cheeked' ships of the past. Typically about 27·4 m (90 ft) long and only 7·3 m (24 ft) in the beam, they usually had two slanting masts and topsail schooner rig, with two jibs.

The Baltimore clippers carried freight down the east coast of America; they were slavers, smugglers and fishing vessels, and they harried the British in the American War of Independence. As a British journalist wrote at the time: 'They daily enter in among our convoys, seize prizes in sight of those that should afford protection, and if pursued put on their sea wings and laugh at the clumsy English pursuers'.

The clipper era

During the mid 19th century several factors combined to spur American shipwrights into building larger and still faster ships. The British government cancelled the East India Company's monopoly of the China tea trade, and followed this in 1849 by repealing the Navigation Acts which until then had denied foreigners the right to carry British cargoes. With fierce competition to be first home with the new season's tea the old 'tea wagons' suddenly lost their appeal. Also in 1849, prospectors clamoured for speedy transportation to the California gold rush. The land journey was hazardous and time consuming, and sea captains had no difficulty filling their ships with those who preferred the sea passage around Cape Horn. Two years later came the Australian gold rush.

Never before had there been such a demand for fast sailing merchantmen. Profits were high, and shipbuilders produced a new type of ship in which building and running expenses, comfort, and even durability and safety were sacrificed for the single virtue of speed; this was the clipper.

43

Above: A traditional fore and aft rigged coastal vessel, the Thames barge.
Right: The French brig 'Brésilien' leaving Le Havre, 1882, by E. Adam.

'Clipper' was a slang work meaning 'fast' or 'racy', and there were no hard and fast rules as to whether a ship was or was not a clipper, or whether it was an 'extreme' or 'sharp' clipper, a 'medium clipper' or a 'half clipper'. However there were certain invariable features, many of them inherited from the Baltimore clipper (which in the usual application of the word was not a clipper but a clipper schooner). They were long in relation to their beam, with raked and finely tapering bow and stern; they carried a towering pyramid of sail, and they were 'full rigged ships'—i.e. they carried a full complement of square sails on each mast as well as the usual jibs, staysails, spankers and stun'sails of East Indiamen like *Essex*.

Challenge, built by William H. Webb of New York in 1853, is an example of a medium clipper. She was 70·26 m (230·5 ft) long, 13·26 m (43·5 ft) in the beam, 8·38 m (27·5 ft) deep, and of 2,006 registered tons (this is a measure of capacity, not weight). Overall her mainmast extended to a height of 70·1 m (230 ft), and she carried some 10,686 m² (115,027 ft²) of sail.

The more famous *Lightning*, constructed by the most renowned of American clipper builders, Donald McKay of Boston, was of the extreme type, with a length of 74·37 m (244 ft), a beam of 13·41 m (44 ft), a depth of 7 m (23 ft), and a registered tonnage of just 1,468. She was particularly 'hollow' at the bows. On her maiden voyage she justified her promise, sailing 702 km (436 miles) in 24 hours—an average speed of just over 15·5 knots.

In 1853 McKay went on to build the largest wooden sailing ship of all time, *Great Republic*. With four decks, four masts, and steam winches to raise the yards, she was 102 m (335 ft) long and 16·15 m (53 ft) in the beam. American clippers were normally built almost entirely of wood, but to strengthen *Great Republic's* vast hull McKay added a latticework of diagonal iron struts to the frame.

British clippers such as *Thermopylae* and *Cutty Sark* were composite ships, with timber planking on an iron frame, and they were mostly rather smaller and sleeker than the American ships. *Cutty Sark* (length 64·77 m, 212·5 ft; beam 10·87 m, 36 ft) had a length to beam ratio of 5·9:1, compared to *Lightning's* which was smaller at 5·5:1.

Clippers could 'ghost' along in the slightest breeze, and sometimes reached 20 knots in a following wind, completing the voyage from China to London or New York in around 100 days. They could even sail backwards, as one skipper discovered to his advantage by sailing up the Shanghai River one tack bow first, the next stern first. But they were tricky ships to handle, and much depended on distributing the cargo to balance the vessel nicely, and on heaving heavy chains across the deck to trim the ship at sea.

Success in the many ocean races that took place was usually the result of a combination of seamanship, hard work, luck and cunning. Captain Keay of *Ariel* wrote: 'My habit during those weeks was never to undress except for my morning bath, and that often took the place of sleep. The naps I had were of the briefest and were mostly on deck'.

44

Skippers would try to trick rivals by, for example, sending misleading signals or by pretending to drop anchor at dusk and then sailing on after the rival really had anchored.

On one occasion Captain Keay was being shadowed by the rival *Spindthrift*. Almost becalmed off Borneo at dusk, *Spindthrift* stood out to sea. Taking a calculated risk Keay put out his lights, sailed *Ariel* close in to the coast to catch the offshore breeze, and felt his way along through the night to win a considerable lead.

In the last resort it was the right balance of seamanship and daring that counted, and the feel for the ships that Keay so clearly had. These qualities are much in evidence in this extract from one of his letters:

Ariel was a perfect beauty to every nautical man who saw her; in symmetrical grace and proportion of hull, spars, sails, rigging and finish, she satisfied the eye and put all in love with her without exception. The curve of stem, figurehead and entrance, the easy sheer and graceful lines of the hull seemed grown and finished as life takes shape and beauty; the proportion and stand of her masts and yards were all perfect. On deck there was the same complete good taste; roomy flush decks with pure white bulwark panels, delicately bordered with green and minutely touched in the centre with azure and vermilion . . . *Ariel* often went 11 and 12 knots sharp

on a bowline, and in fair winds 14, 15 and 16 knots for hours together. The best day's work in south latitude, running east, was 340 nautical miles by observation, and that was done by carrying all plain sail except mizen royal, the wind being three or four points on the quarter.

The golden age of the clipper ship was brief. Even before the first clippers were built, steamships had made their appearance, and with the opening of the Suez Canal, and of the transcontinental railway across America, in the 1860s the clipper's turn of speed lost its initial significance. However, they were fine vessels, much too good to scrap, so they were refitted and changed their old role as greyhounds to become workhorses of the oceans undertaking various tasks.

The story of *Cutty Sark* is typical. Launched in 1869, she made eight voyages as a tea clipper. In 1880 her sail plan was reduced to make her easier and therefore cheaper to work, and she entered the

Below left: The captain of the steamship 'Ruapehu' ordered full steam ahead, but was unable to prevent the sailing ship 'Turakina' passing him. This remarkable duel occurred in 1895. Both ships were owned by the New Zealand Shipping Company, which commissioned this painting by Frank H. Mason. It is interesting to note that even at this late date steamships still carried auxiliary sails.
Below: The clipper 'Cutty Sark' in dry dock at Greenwich, England.

Australian wool trade—in 1887–8 making a record passage from Sydney to London in 71 days. Then in 1895 she was purchased by a Portuguese company, which renamed her *Ferreira*. Dismasted in a storm in 1916, she was rerigged as a barquentine (square sails on the foremast only), and continued in service until 1922 when she was bought by an English captain who restored her clipper rig. After many years at Falmouth, England as a training ship she was finally fully restored and placed on show in dry dock at Greenwich, London.

The end of an era

Despite advances in steamship design, the latter part of the 19th century saw the development of a new type of sailing ship which fulfilled the shipping companies' desire for size, economy and ease of maintenance. On certain runs sailing vessels were still faster than steamships; they did not need a chain of bunkering stations en route, and with pens of livestock on board for fresh meat, they could stay at sea for months on end. The new windjammers, as they were called, carried Chilean nitrate around Cape Horn; they shipped grain from Australia, and guano from Peru.

Builders of steam ships had already shown that iron was both stronger and, for a given hull size, lighter than wood. The introduction of steel brought a further 15 per cent reduction in weight. These factors allowed shipwrights to give the new metal sailing ships a much increased length to beam ratio. So they built longer ships, which in turn made the addition of a fourth mast necessary to balance the sail plan. Massive though they were, these sleek 'four posters' proved even faster than the clipper. *Lancing*, the fastest of all, was curiously a converted steamship. Built in Glasgow, Scotland for the Compagnie Générale Transatlantique, she spent 22 years as a steamship and a further 36 under sail before finally reaching the scrapyard in 1924. The last, and at 123·4 m (405 ft) the longest of the four masted full rigged ships, she achieved a remarkable 22 knots, and during a passage between New York and Melbourne, Australia, she averaged a speed of 18 knots for a full 72 hours.

The most usual rig of these tall ships of the last days of sail was the three or four masted barque, on which the after mast was fore and aft rigged and the rest square rigged. This, together with the use of steam winches to hoist the yards, and a general simplification and mechanization of the running rigging, enabled a smaller crew to run the ship. The barquentine, with square sails only on the foremast, provided still greater economies but less speed.

Seeking running economy in size, some European shipbuilders turned to five masters. The German P-Line's *Preussen* of 1902, a full rigger, and the *France*

II of 1911, a barque, were two of the most famous, and were the largest sailing ships ever built. *Preussen* displaced 11,328 tonnes, was 146·9 m (482 ft) long overall, 16·15 m (53 ft) in the beam, and carried an immense sail area of 5,574 m² (60,000 ft²). Yet she required a crew of just 48 compared to a tea clipper's 35 or 40, and carried roughly four times the weight of cargo per man. This ratio applied in the case of, for example, the *Cutty Sark*.

Then there were the freaks with over five masts, including *City of Sydney* and *E. R. Sterling*, six masted barquentines, and the ill-fated American schooner *Thomas W. Lawson*, with no less than seven masts but a crew of only 16. Her sail area was scarcely more than one third that of the earlier and vastly smaller clippers, and she proved slow and awkward to handle. Launched in 1902, she capsized and sank in the English Channel in 1908.

Tall ships today

By the start of World War II the day of the tall ships was over, but today they are enjoying something of a renaissance. The *Sir Winston Churchill*, a three masted topsail schooner, was launched as recently as 1966. She, like others in countries around the world, is a training ship for cadets of the navy and merchant marine. Even in this age of mechanization and automation, or perhaps one should say especially in such an age, the experience gained from working on a tall ship is both rewarding and valuable.

From time to time, tall ships gather for an ocean race, and their grace and beauty appeal to the general public as much as to sailing enthusiasts—while businessmen are reconsidering their economic virtues. On account of the need to conserve energy and rocketing fuel bills, shipping companies are beginning to wonder whether the sailing ship does not after all still have a place in the nuclear age.

The German engineer Wilhelm Prölss has invented a computerized six masted square rigger, the Dynaship. The traditional maze of rigging has vanished from sight, leaving the decks free for easy access to the holds, and cutting down wind resistance. The sails are set and trimmed by cables running inside the hollow masts, and are controlled by one man in a computerized control room. The masts can be rotated to set the sails at the best angle, and wind tunnel tests have shown that a ship built on these lines is likely to be some 60 per cent more efficient than the sailing ships of the golden age.

Other people, including experts in America, have proposed more conventional sailing merchantmen. Perhaps in the future we shall see, on certain runs at least, a revival of sail.

Right: The Polish training ship 'Dar Pomorza'. A three masted full rigged ship, she carries a permanent crew of 30, and 100 trainees.

From ironclad to dreadnought

During the 150 years before the Battle of Trafalgar warships altered little. But the following 60 years saw a revolution in their propulsion, design, construction and armament. In view of the fact that the first commercially successful steamboat services started operating before Trafalgar, the revolution took a long time getting under way. But naval authorities, and seamen, are notoriously conservative, and few cared for the idea of raging furnaces on board their wooden warships. There were other reasons for their hesitancy. Early steamships were propelled by huge paddle wheels at either side, roughly amidships, and although naval experts appreciated the tactical and strategic advantages of independence from the wind, they saw that the paddle wheels were dangerously vulnerable to enemy fire, and that they and the engines that

turned them took up a good deal of valuable gun space.

First in the field was the American steam powered warship *Demologos*, built in 1812 to combat the British blockade in the war of that year. Designed by the American inventor and leading pioneer of steamboats, Robert Fulton, *Demologos* was a mobile floating gun platform with many novel features including twin hulls. The single paddle wheel was placed between the hulls, while one hull held the engine and the other the boilers and funnel. Armed with 30 guns firing 14·5 kg (32 lb) shot preheated in the furnace, and capable of over six knots, she might have proved an effective weapon. However she arrived too late to take part in the war, and was accidentally destroyed by fire in 1829.

The first steam ships to enter naval service were small steam tugs. Their main job was to tow the large sailing men of war in and out of harbour, but they occasionally fought as warships. During the 1820s the New York Harbor steam tug USS *Sea Gull* was sent into action against pirates in the West Indies.

The French navy led the way in fitting auxiliary steam engines to sailing warships. But the huge paddle boxes looked as if they had been added as an afterthought and this was indeed the case. And to aggravate the problems already mentioned, the paddles and their boxes interfered with the ships' sailing abilities.

It began to look as if steam power might have to wait until it was powerful and reliable enough to be used on its own, without sails. However, the outlook changed when in 1843 the US Navy launched the world's first screw propelled steam-plus-sail warship, *Princeton*. The marine propeller had been developed by among others the Swedish inventor John Ericsson, and taken by him to the British Admiralty in 1836. They turned it down, on the theory that a propeller rotating at the stern would simply drive the ship around in circles.

A US naval officer, Captain R. F. Stockton, invited Ericsson to America. There he found a more progressive attitude, and his propeller was tried on the steam frigates *Princeton* and *Mississippi*. Both craft had another novel feature: telescopic funnels. The idea was that they could approach a hostile vessel in the guise of a sailing ship.

The acceptance of screw propulsion by the US Navy spurred its development in Europe. In Britain the Admiralty first arranged a tug of war to persuade them once and for all of the screw's superiority. This strange contest occurred in 1845, when two ships of equal size and power—one, HMS *Rattler*, screw propelled, the other, HMS *Alecto*, paddle driven— were lashed together stern to stern. With both ships

Left: The 'Monitor', 1862. The first turret ship, she finally ended the era of the broadside.

at full steam ahead, *Rattler* towed *Alecto* away at a convincing 2·8 knots.

In France the keel was laid in 1848 for the first screw propelled battleship, *Napoléon*. Built of wood and fully rigged, she stood at the bridge between two eras. In looks she was remarkably similar to a ship of the line of 50 years earlier. But 671 kW (900 hp) engines and screw propulsion gave her a speed—with sails furled—of 11 knots, and she was equipped with the latest cannon firing explosive shells.

The first ironclads

The introduction of shells, which could tear wooden ships apart, as the Russians had shown convincingly at the Battle of Sinope in 1853, brought two new factors to the naval arms race: the development of larger and more powerful shells, and the concurrent evolution of armour to give some protection from the shells.

Here again, France and America led the way. As early as 1842 Dupuy de Lôme, designer of *Napoléon*, advocated iron warships, and in the same year the US Secretary of the Navy, Abel P. Ipshur, said: 'It seems no longer doubtful that iron ships will answer all the purposes of coast and harbor defense, and probably also of ocean cruising. It is the wish of this department to construct as many vessels as possible of this material'. During the same period the British experimented by firing solid shot at iron plating (the resultant hole was more difficult to plug than that in a timber hull), while at the same time fitting shell firing guns into wooden ships—a remarkable contradiction between the old and new philosophies, and one which was fostered by the general public's fierce hostility to metal warships.

The French produced the first ironclad warships, three 'floating batteries'—*Devastation*, *Tonnante* and *Lave*—which bombarded Russian fortifications during the Crimean War. Their already massive timbers were clad with a layer of iron plating 114·3 mm (4·5 in) thick, which effectively protected them from the shellfire of the period. It was of course only a matter of time before improvements in armament would render this sort of protection inadequate. However the French proceeded to build the world's first seagoing ironclad, *Gloire*. Displacing 5707 tonnes (5617 tons), and measuring 78 m (255·7 ft) in length and 17 m (55·7 ft) in the beam, *Gloire* attained a speed of 13·5 knots and carried 36 164 mm (6·46 in) guns. Still essentially a wooden ship, she was fitted with armour plating like her predecessors at Crimea.

Britain promptly countered with the world's first

Above left: The 'Agincourt', 1868, one of the longest single screw warships.
Left: The 'Captain', an early British turret ship. Her tall masts were her downfall—she capsized in a gale with the loss of all hands.

all iron seagoing warship, *Warrior*. Laid down in 1859, launched on 29 December 1860, and superior in speed and firepower to *Gloire*, she was truly the first of a new generation. As her gunnery officer wrote: 'It certainly was not appreciated then that this, our first armour clad ship of war, would cause a fundamental change in what had been in vogue for something like a thousand years'. *Warrior* was much larger than *Gloire*, with an overall length of 128 m (420 ft) and a displacement of 9358 tonnes (9210 tons).

Yet even *Warrior* had not fully broken with the past. Her steam engine and screw propeller gave her a top speed of 14·5 knots, but she was still a full rigged three master. And heavily armed as she was, she remained a broadside ship. Her guns were, as of old, arranged along either side, and could only be aimed by 'aiming' the entire ship.

'Monitor' v. 'Merrimac'

The final break with the past came in America during the Civil War. A variety of novel craft fought in this conflict, including primitive submarines, balloon 'carriers' (the balloons were used for observation), ironclad ramships and little 'Davids' which carried a 'torpedo' on an outrigger at the bow. But none of these was stranger than the *Monitor*. Designed by John Ericsson (of screw propeller fame) at the request of the United States' Congress, *Monitor* was built at record speed in 100 days, launched on 23 January 1862, and promptly nicknamed the 'cheesebox on a raft'. The 'raft', *Monitor's* hull, was 52·5 m (172 ft) long, 12·65 m (41·5 ft) wide and displaced around 1000 tonnes. Built like a box, with a completely flat deck and straight sides, and a freeboard of less then 1 m (3·28 ft), she was of all iron construction and heavily armoured. The steam engine, fitted down in the hold below the waterline, drove two propellers. But the 'cheesebox' was her most significant feature, comprising a 6 m (20 ft) diameter revolving gun turret (itself heavily armour plated) mounting two 11 in guns. There was nothing new in the turret idea, and indeed the British navy had been toying with it in recent years, but it had never actually been employed before in a full scale mobile warship.

On 9 March 1862 *Monitor* fought a historic duel in Hampton Roads with the Confederate ironclad *Merrimac* The latter, originally a wooden steam frigate owned by the Federal forces and sunk by them in their retreat from the Norfolk Naval Shipyard, had been raised by the Confederates and given a slanting metal superstructure made from railway tracks. Her ten guns fired through ports in this tank like superstructure, and on 8 March she sank two wooden Federal ships with ease and complete immunity from their guns.

In the Battle of Hampton Roads *Monitor* and *Merrimac* hammered away at each other for hours

53

until *Monitor's* ammunition ran out, and *Merrimac* steamed away, her gunnery officer exclaiming: 'I can do as much damage by snapping my fingers'. *Monitor* was in fact desperately unseaworthy; she almost sank en route to Hampton Roads, and actually did sink on her next sea voyage. But she had vividly demonstrated the advantage of revolving gun turrets. And the duel—the first between ironclads—at the same time made apparent to even the most conservative the necessity of iron armour, of steam power, and of a deck uncluttered by masts and rigging.

Within days the British Admiralty had a large 131 gun warship cut down, armoured and fitted with turrets. And navies around the world turned to the development of all-metal, steam-powered, ocean-going warships.

The development of the dreadnoughts

The first of the new generation of turret battleships was Britain's HMS *Monarch*, 1869. Still combining sail and steam, her top speed was close to 15 knots. She mounted four 12 in guns in two central turrets. *Monarch* was succeeded four years later by the sail-less HMS *Devastation*, of 9480 tonnes (9330 tons), described at the time as 'an impregnable piece of Vauban fortification with bastions mounted upon a fighting coal mine', and more recently as an 'armoured citadel'. The 'coal mine' referred to *Devastation's* massive bunkers, which held 1625 tonnes (1600 tons) of coal. Her four guns, in two turrets, each weighed 35·56 tonnes (35 tons), while her armour, a minimum of 203·2 mm (8 in) thick weighed over 2500 tonnes.

Devastation set a trend for the massively armed and armoured battleships of the next 20 years or so. These included the Italian 10,000 tonne *Duilio* and *Dandolo*, with four 381 mm (15 in) 100 tonne guns and steel armour up to 536 mm (21·5 in) thick; the French *Formidable*, and finally the British *Inflexible*, with a maximum armour thickness of 610 mm (24 in) and four 16 in guns.

This brief race for massive armour and armament took place in a vacuum when there were no large scale naval actions in which to test the ships. Had there been a fleet action, officers would doubtless have found their super ships dangerously low in the water (necessary with such heavy guns), and their guns powerful but hopelessly inaccurate and slow to reload. Fortunately developments in naval architecture, metallurgy, and gunnery made possible the birth of the second generation of battleships. Representative of this new type were America's Indiana class of 1891, Britain's Majestic class, and the German Kaiser battleships.

With steel armour, higher freeboard and trimmer lines, these ships were more manoeuvrable and seaworthy. And they mounted the new lighter breech loading guns in a more flexible mixed array. The Indiana class, for example, had large turrets fore and aft, each with two 13 in guns, four smaller turrets between with a total of eight 8 in guns, as well as smaller guns for defence from the new torpedo boats, and six torpedo tubes.

The theory behind this mixed armament was that the big guns should aim to sink a hostile ship, while the smaller and quicker firing weapons raked its superstructure. However the increased range and accuracy of the big guns, and of torpedoes, soon brought this theory into question, and during the first major fleet action between battleships the question was quickly resolved. The action, between

Above left: The British turret ship 'Devastation', 1873, the first seagoing battleship powered by steam alone.
Above: The 'Dreadnought', 1906, the first of the all big gun battleships, and the first with steam turbine engines.

Russia and Japan on 27 May 1905, took place in the Straits of Tsushima, Japan. The Japanese ships began firing at a range of 8230 m (9000 yd), and their 12 in shells soon dispatched the Russian battleship *Oslyabya*.

Although the Japanese and American navies were the first to lay down all-big-gun battleships, the British were the first to launch one, and her name— *Dreadnought*—was soon adopted for all battleships of her type. Armed with ten 12 in guns in five turrets, *Dreadnought* at once made obsolete all other battleships, including her companions in the British fleet.

World War I battleships and cruisers

Dreadnought initiated a world wide arms race on the grand scale, culminating in super dreadnoughts such as the British Queen Elizabeth class, the German ships *Baden* and *Bayern*, and the American *Oklahoma* and *Nevada*. Although designed for large scale fleet action, dreadnought battleships only confronted each other en masse once during World War I, at the Battle of Jutland in May 1916. Mastery of the seas was vital to Britain's survival, and although her battle fleet was superior to Germany's, she could no more afford to take risks than her opponent. Hence a major fleet action was deliberately avoided until, at Jutland, Germany attempted to lure, trap and destroy a significant part of the British fleet. The battle was inconclusive, both sides claiming victory. Britain lost 14 ships and 6274 men, Germany 11 ships and 2545 men. But at the end of the day the German fleet was trapped in harbour and remained there for the duration of the war.

Too big and expensive to risk in a massive confrontation, the dreadnoughts ranged the oceans in small groups, assisted by battle cruisers, cruisers and smaller ships. Taking the place of the frigates of the ship of the line era, cruisers were by 1900 of two main types: armoured and light. Designed for raiding actions on merchant ships and as scouts to the main battle fleet, armoured cruisers included the German 15,240 tonne (15,000 ton) *Blücher*, the American Washington class, and the Italian Vittorio Emanuele class. Armament usually consisted of 8 in and 12 in guns, and top speed was between 21 and 25 knots. With the appearance of the larger and better armed battle cruisers of World War I the armoured cruiser became obsolete.

Battle cruisers, favoured mainly by the British and German navies, equalled the firepower of the dreadnoughts but were less heavily armoured and hence lighter and faster. Britain's HMS *Invincible* (1908) and her sister ships *Inflexible* and *Indomitable* had a remarkable speed of 27 knots, while German battle cruisers such as the *von der Tann*, *Lützow* and *Goeben* were almost as fast and decidedly better armoured.

Light, or unprotected, cruisers, armed with guns of up to 6 in calibre, played an important role as scouts and patrol boats throughout the war, and notably at Jutland. Fast enough to evade the guns of battle cruisers and armoured cruisers, they had little or no armour but were adequately armed for light raiding duties.

55

HMS 'Dreadnought', 1906. The largest and fastest battleship of her time. The diagram top right shows the layout of her armament, and that six big guns could fire forward and aft and eight on the beam.

Displacement	18,187 tonnes (17,900 tons)
Length	160·6 m (527 ft)
Beam	25 m (82 ft)
Draught	8 m (26·5 ft)
Engines	Direct drive turbines with a shaft power of 17,151 kW (23,000 hp).
Speed	21 knots
Crew	About 750
Armament	10 304·8 mm (12 in) guns
	24 5·44 kg (12 lb) guns
	5 457·2 mm (18 in) torpedo tubes
Armour	Maximum thickness 279·4 mm (11 in)

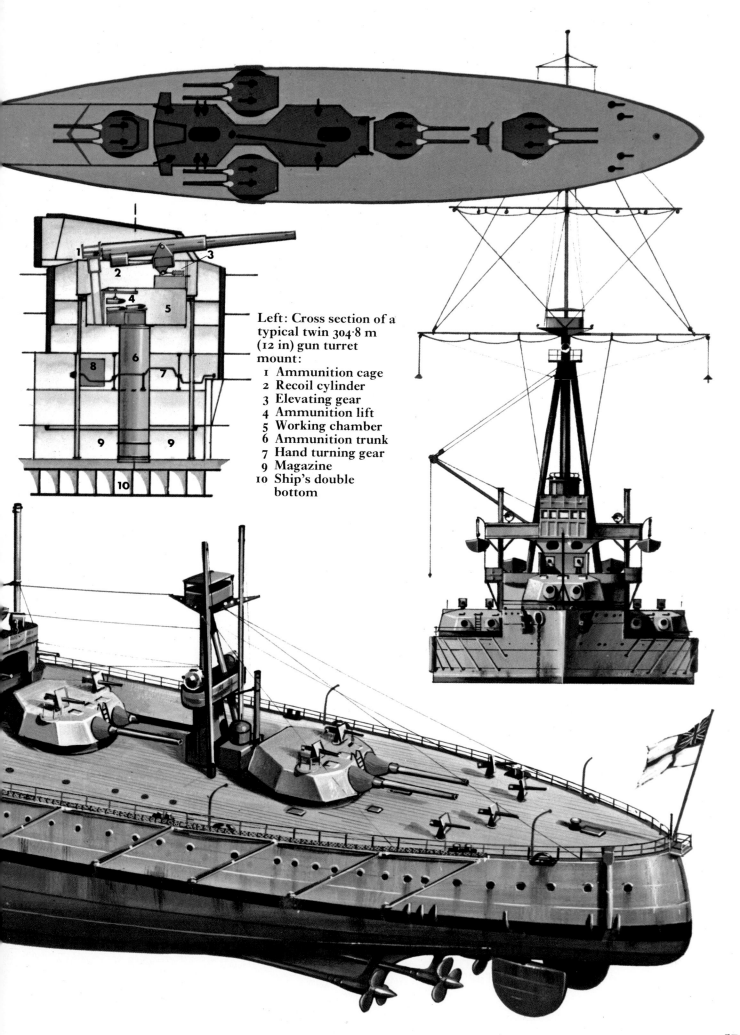

Left: Cross section of a typical twin 304·8 m (12 in) gun turret mount:
1 Ammunition cage
2 Recoil cylinder
3 Elevating gear
4 Ammunition lift
5 Working chamber
6 Ammunition trunk
7 Hand turning gear
9 Magazine
10 Ship's double bottom

Right: Four scenes of the Battle of Jutland. The largest shows the British battle line firing. The three small pictures show ship to ship actions, and place the ships much closer together than they actually were.

58

Torpedo boats, destroyers and submarines

Starting as an explosive charge fixed to a spar at the bow of a small warship or submarine, and progressing to a towed device pulled across the enemy's bows, the torpedo had advanced by the 1890s into a weapon with a 136 kg (300 lb) warhead and a range of around 914 m (1000 yd). The first torpedo boats, tiny craft displacing a mere 20 or 39 tonnes, were intended for inshore and harbour action. The Royal Navy produced a torpedo boat carrier which could lower the boats over the side when the scene of action was reached, but this was clearly an unsatisfactory approach, and soon navies began laying down larger seagoing torpedo boats which could sail with the fleet. Known intially as torpedo catchers and later as torpedo boat destroyers, they combined offensive and defensive roles, being equipped to attack enemy ships with torpedoes and to run down enemy torpedo boats.

Carrying the navy's most lethal weapon, and capable of sustained high speeds, the new destroyers became the workhouse among warships—defending the fleet, darting in on lightning attacks and escaping before the enemy had time to react, convoying merchantmen, and hunting and destroying the new submarines. Typical destroyers of World War I displaced around 1000 tonnes, measured some 85 m (280 ft) in length, and sped through the water at an unprecedented 30 to 35 knots. Their 457 to 533 mm (18 to 21 in) torpedoes could destroy a dreadnought at a range of 6400 m (7000 yd).

The first submarine used in combat, David Bushnell's *Turtle* of 1776, resembled an upended turtle, and was hand powered by its single occupant. *Hunley*, the first to sink an enemy ship, in 1864, (the Union warship *Housatonic*), was also hand cranked, and was itself destroyed in the explosion. However, by 1900 effective submarines had been built in America (the *Holland*) and France (the *Narval*), with petrol engines for surface use and electric motors for underwater propulsion.

Despite the widely held view that submarines were 'underhand, unfair and damned un-English' (the words are those of an English admiral), their development forged ahead and by the outbreak of World War I Britain had 75 submarines, France 67, Germany 30 and America 39. During the war Germany, unable to match the British on the surface, concentrated on submarine warfare with devastating results. Their fleet, like those of Britain and other countries, consisted mainly of 61 m (200 ft) craft displacing less than 1000 tonnes when surfaced. But they also possessed eight Deutschland class U-boats 95 m (315 ft) long, with a surface speed of 13 knots and a submerged speed of 7 knots.

Right: The Soviet cruiser 'Aurora', preserved at Leningrad to commemorate her part in the 1917 October Revolution.

60

World War II and beyond

The last battleships

During World War I the arrival of aeroplanes had brought an entirely new dimension into naval warfare, and after the war far sighted theorists argued that the usefulness of the battleship was at an end. It had done little actual fighting in the Great War, and now it was too large and too vulnerable to attack from the air. However, advocates of the dreadnought type battleship remained undeterred, and in the immediate post war years America, Japan and Britain initiated massive building programmes. Japan and America, who had emerged from the war as powerful industrial nations, were the principal protagonists, each fearing the other's intentions in the Pacific. Britain, impoverished by the conflict, tagged along behind.

Japan proposed giants armed with 18 in guns. America countered by authorizing battleships of over 40,000 tonnes, and Britain followed suit. An arms race of crippling expense seemed under way until the Washington Treaty of 1922 imposed limitations in size and number to the ships of the signatory nations' fleets. This provided a temporary respite during which the world's navies concentrated on rebuilding and refitting existing ships, or replacing them as they became obsolete. The Washington Treaty expired in 1930 and its successor, the London Naval Treaty, was signed in 1936. But by then international tension was mounting, Germany had launched her notorious 'pocket battleships', and soon all the great powers laid down new super dreadnoughts.

The pocket battleships were claimed to meet the heavy cruiser specifications of the Washington Treaty, which had imposed a limit of 10,160 tonnes (10,000 tons). In fact they displaced nearer 12,000 tonnes, and carried a main armament of six 11 in guns. Their diesel engines gave them a speed of 26 knots, and an impressive radius of action of some 16,000 km (10,000 miles). The pocket battleships were intended for merchant raiding, and Germany laid down the battleships *Bismarck* and *Tirpitz* with the same role

Left: A detail from Eurich's painting 'Bombardment of a coast by HM ships 'King George V' and 'Duke of York'.'

in mind. Launched in 1941, *Bismarck* displaced 53,444 tonnes (52,600 tons) at full load, carried eight 15 in guns in four twin turrets and twelve 5·9 in guns. She was unusually strongly built and heavily armoured. Claims that she was unsinkable were soon disproved, but the story of her brief career reveals both the strength and the weakness of the battleship. Her presence on the high seas was considered so dangerous that Britain deployed 19 major warships against her in a chase that lasted almost five days (23–27 May 1941). Engaged first by the battle cruiser *Hood* and the battleship *Prince of Wales*, *Bismarck* survived hits from *Prince of Wales*, sank *Hood* and forced *Prince of Wales* to withdraw. In the ensuing hunt *Bismarck* was hit by five airborne and seaborne torpedoes and survived a further 24 hour pounding from the guns of the battleships *King George V* and *Rodney*, before finally being sunk by three torpedoes from the cruiser *Dorsetshire*.

Rodney and her sister ship *Nelson*, 1927, were the most powerful of Britain's battleships, with a main armament of nine 16 in guns in three turrets. *King George V* and *Prince of Wales*, two of a group of five built between 1937 and 1942, were considerably larger but less heavily armed. Displacing 44,706 tonnes (44,000 tons) and with an overall length of 227 m (745 ft), they mounted ten 14 in guns.

To combat the dangers of air attack *Prince of Wales*, like other battleships of the time, bristled with anti-aircraft guns. But these failed to save her from destruction by Japanese torpedo-carrying aircraft in December 1941. The lesson, reinforcing the one given three days earlier by Japan's airborne attack on the American fleet in Pearl Harbor, was quickly learned. The battleship destroyers of World War II were not other battleships, as had been expected by many, but aircraft. Forced into a secondary role by the aircraft carrier, battleships became merchant raiders and convoy escorts; they bombarded shore positions and they sailed with the aircraft carriers, providing supporting anti-aircraft fire and added protection from surface attack. They were given thicker armour, especially on the deck and turrets,

The Japanese super dreadnought 'Yamato', 1941. 'Yamato' and her sister ship 'Musashi' were the largest battleships of all time. Seen here in different stages of her career, 'Yamato' began life with 25 25 mm (0·98 in) anti aircraft guns and had amassed a total of 146 of this calibre alone before she was sunk on 6 April 1945. The immense strength of her armour is shown in the fact that she received direct hits from 12 torpedoes and 7 bombs before finally exploding. Her hull was subdivided into 1147 watertight compartments.

Displacement (full load)	73,977 tonnes (72,809 tons)
Length	263 m (863 ft)
Beam	38·7 m (127 ft)
Draught	10·7 m (35 ft)
Engines	Steam turbines with a shaft power of 111,855 kW (150,000 hp).
Speed	27 knots
Crew	2500
Armament	9 457 mm (18 in) guns
	12 155 mm (6·1 in) guns
	12 127 mm (5 in) guns
	146 25 mm (0·98 in) AA guns
	4 13 mm (0·51 in) guns
	6 aircraft
Armour	Deck, 212 mm (8·35 in)
	Sides 410 mm (16·14 in)
	Turrets, 650 mm (25·6 in)

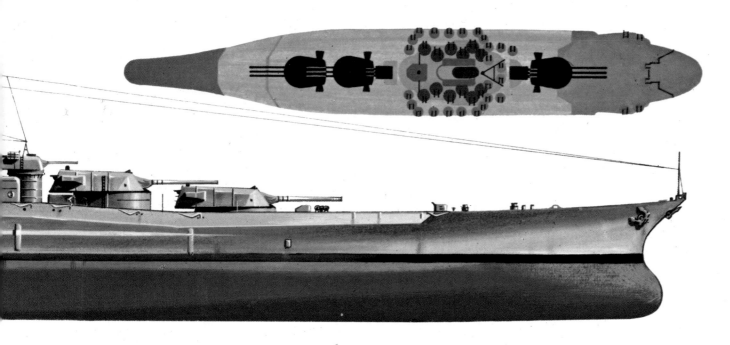

Right: 'Yamato's' after flight deck, with catapults for launching the aircraft. These were Aichi 'Jakes' and Mitsubishi 'Petes'.

and they reached their culmination in the great American and Japanese battleships of the war.

The US Navy's Iowa class ships *New Jersey*, *Iowa*, *Missouri* and *Wisconsin*, the most formidable of all Allied battleships, displaced 58,524 tonnes (57,600 tons) at full load. Some 270·4 m (887·25 ft) long and 32·9 m (108 ft) in the beam, they dwarfed the original *Dreadnought* in size and armament, mounting nine 16 in guns, twenty 5 in, eighty 40 mm, forty-eight 20 mm, and carrying four aeroplanes. That all four survived the war was a tribute to their builders, their crews, and to the naval strategy that ensured adequate air support.

Their Japanese rivals *Yamato* and *Musashi* were less fortunate. Japan failed to maintain air superiority, so although these, the greatest of all battleships, were completed in 1941 and 1942, they spent much of the war in hiding. The strength of their armour was unprecedented. The 212 mm (8·35 in) deck armour could withstand a 907 kg (2000 lb) bomb dropped from 3050 m (10,000 ft), while the 410 mm (16·14 in) side armour was almost—but not quite—unassailable. Yet when they finally emerged in 1945 to face the American carrier fleet they did not stand a chance. *Musashi* sank after 16 direct hits by torpedoes and 11 by bombs (see elsewhere in this chapter for *Yamato's* details and specifications).

Aircraft carriers

Although the American civilian pilot Eugene Ely had demonstrated the possibility of taking off from and landing on the deck of a ship as early as 1910–11, aircraft carriers of World War I were makeshift affairs. Most carried seaplanes. These were lowered over the side to take off from the water, and had to be recovered by the reverse procedure at the end of each mission. Later in the war techniques had progressed to the stage where wheeled aircraft could take off from deck, but not land on it. They had to be recovered from the sea, a time consuming process for which the carrier had to stop.

After experiments with flight decks fore and aft, the British developed the first aircraft carrier with an unobstructed flight deck running the length of the ship. Named *Argus*, she was a converted merchant ship, and was completed too late to enter active service.

Argus was followed in the early 1920s by the first two purpose built carriers, the Japanese *Hosho* and the British *Hermes*. The basic structure had emerged, with the aircraft stored in hangars below deck and raised to flight deck level by lifts. The British went on to evolve the island design, in which the navigating bridge and funnels were offset on the starboard side, thereby fully clearing the flight deck of obstructions and smoke. Britain's Admiral Fisher, whose vision and

Left: Small guns on board the American battleship 'Arkansas'.

67

German U-boats of World War II. The four types
illustrated are, from top to bottom, the II-B,
the VII, the IX-B and the XXI. The II-B, an early
coastal submarine in service at the beginning of
the war, was armed with three 533 mm (21 in) torpedo
tubes and carried six torpedoes or eight mines. The
Type VII, the principal oceangoing U-boat in the
war of the Atlantic, had a surface speed of 17·25 knots
and could maintain 7·5 knots when submerged.
It carried five torpedo tubes, four forward and one aft.
Cruising range on the surface was 10,460 km
(6500 miles) at 12 knots. A variant, the Type VII-F,
a stretched version 77·6 m (254·75 ft) in length, served
as a submarine supply ship. The Type IX-B was a long
range craft with a cruising range of 13,035 km
(8100 miles).

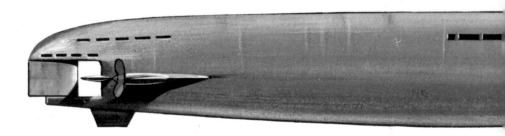

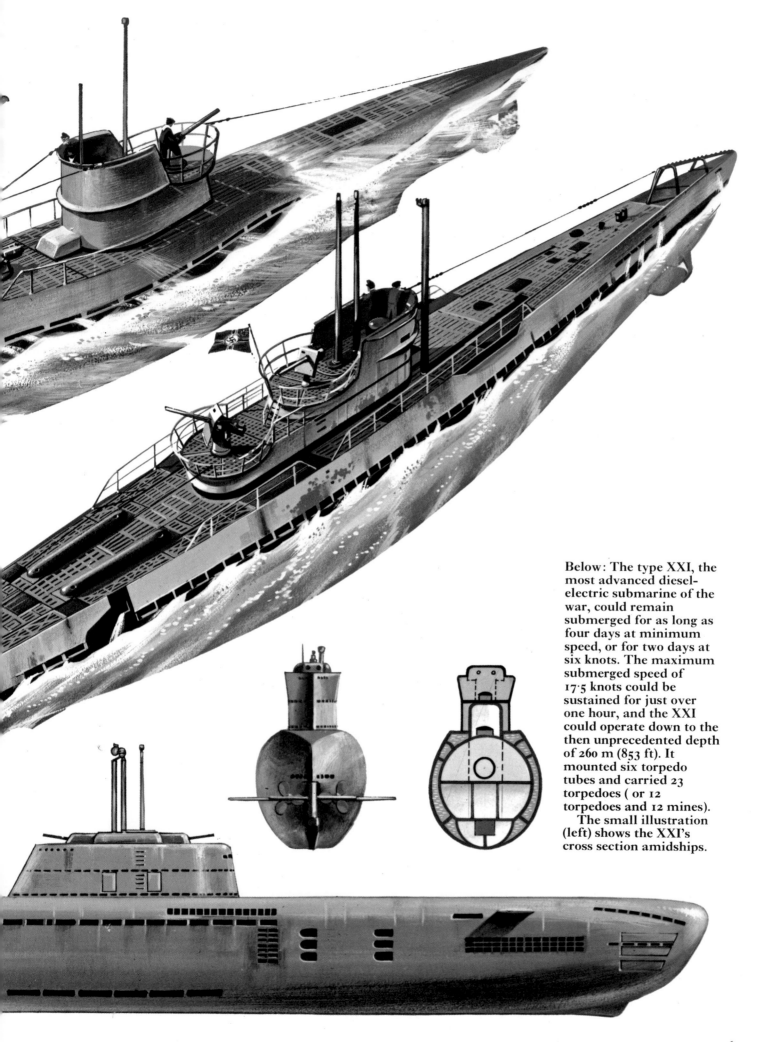

Below: The type XXI, the most advanced diesel-electric submarine of the war, could remain submerged for as long as four days at minimum speed, or for two days at six knots. The maximum submerged speed of 17·5 knots could be sustained for just over one hour, and the XXI could operate down to the then unprecedented depth of 260 m (853 ft). It mounted six torpedo tubes and carried 23 torpedoes (or 12 torpedoes and 12 mines).

The small illustration (left) shows the XXI's cross section amidships.

energy had led to the creation of the first *Dreadnought*, wrote in 1920: 'To build battleships so long as cheaper craft can destroy them is merely to breed cats unable to catch rats or mice . . . Why keep any of the present lot? All you want is the present naval side of the air force!—that's the future navy!' However, his country was to be left behind in the succeeding years. It was the navies of Japan and America, facing each other across the Pacific, who took the lead in carrier development in the late 1920s and 1930s, and who assimilated the implications for naval strategy and tactics. While Britain continued to regard carriers as secondary to battleships, Japan and America appreciated their true significance and evolved specialized dive bombers, torpedo bombers and fighters to operate from them. Thus although Britain retained superiority in numbers, the Japanese and American ships were far better fighting units. Typical British carriers at the start of World War II such as the 22,353 tonne (22,000 ton) *Ark Royal* carried 60 aircraft, while Japanese ships like the 16,256 tonne (16,000 ton) *Hiryu* carried 73, and the American *Enterprise* held 80. *Enterprise* and her sister ship *Yorktown* displaced 20,320 tonnes (20,000 tons), measured 246·6 m (809 ft) in length and had a top speed of 34 knots. Britain's later *Illustrious* class, heavily armoured though they were and displacing 23,369 tonnes (23,000 tons) carried just 36 aircraft, while America's *Essex* class carried 100.

The progress of World War II quickly revealed the strength and importance of aircraft carriers. Carrier based Japanese aircraft bombarded the American fleet at Pearl Harbor, and at the Battle of the Coral Sea in May 1942 the Japanese and American fleets fought a major naval action without once sighting each other. At Midway a month later Japan lost four carriers in a battle which gave America command of the Pacific. In the ensuing years American carriers cleared remaining Japanese naval opposition in the Pacific, operating in task forces made up of three or four carriers, six or seven battleships and a bevy of destroyers. The success of these actions enabled American and British carriers to sail unharmed into Japanese waters in 1945. There they provided aerial support to the battleships, which proceeded to bombard the Japanese coast with impunity.

Wartime experience led America to adopt the British philosophy of more heavily armoured carriers, while the British belatedly appreciated the importance of greater striking power. Britain's Audacious class, laid down in 1941, were designed to carry a force of 100 aircraft, while America's Midway class had an armoured flight deck. These huge ships, commissioned too late to take part in the war against Japan, carried 137 aircraft, displaced 45,722 tonnes (45,000 tons), and could maintain a speed of 33 knots. They measured 295 m (968 ft) in length and 34·4 m (113 ft)

in the beam.

The advent of jet aircraft in the post war years led to several innovations in carrier design. Catapult assisted takeoff had been a feature of carriers from the earliest years, as had braking wires across the flight deck. These engaged with retractable hooks on the aircraft to provide rapid braking. The new jets were slower to accelerate at takeoff, and had a higher landing speed. The introduction of steam powered catapults solved the launching problem, but safe landing necessitated a more radical development. The usual arrangement in the propeller era had been to divide the flight deck into a longer aft section for takeoff and landing, and a shorter forward section for parking. The two were divided by a crash barrier which brought any plane that failed to pick up the landing wire to a halt—an inadequate procedure for a heavy jet fighter with a high landing speed.

The angled flight deck solved this problem. With a flight deck angled or canted out from the fore and aft line of the ship, aircraft have a longer run, and if they fail to catch the landing wire they can simply fly on, circle and try again. The angled flight deck and steam catapult, both British inventions, were quickly adopted by other navies, and are incorporated in the world's latest aircraft carriers, nuclear powered giants such as the USS *Enterprise*, *Nimitz* and *Eisenhower*. *Enterprise*, the longest ever warship (341·3 m, 1123 ft) was launched in 1960, displaces some 86,364 tonnes (85,000 tons), and carries up to 100 aircraft including defence and strike fighters, bombers and helicopters. Her flight deck measures 335·6 m (1101 ft) by 76·8 m (252 ft), and her compact nuclear reactors and absence of oil bunkers free valuable space for aviation fuel and ordnance.

World War II submarines and the convoy system

Submarine technology advanced rapidly in the interwar years. America produced *Argonaut*, a large long range craft armed with four torpedo tubes, two 6 in guns and 60 mines. Britain, France and Japan all experimented with long range merchant raiders carrying seaplanes to extend their hunting and striking abilities. However these underwater carriers proved ineffective in practice, and more conventional submarines played the significant role in World War II. These included the American Gato and Balao classes, 94·9 m (311·5 ft) craft with a surface speed of 20 knots and a submerged ability of 9 knots. Operating at depths of up to 122 m (400 ft), they mounted 10 torpedo tubes and carried 24 torpedoes. Facing them

Right: Allied mastery in the Mediterranean was vital to a successful invasion of Italy. This German photograph, showing the blazing remains of an Allied merchant ship, was taken before that mastery had been attained.

The US aircraft carrier 'Essex', the first of a new class of that name which entered service in the Pacific in 1943. Incorporating an overhanging flight deck to port for extra width, and an outboard lift (visible amidships in the lower illustration), these carriers were superior to their Japanese counterparts. With them the Americans were able to clear the Pacific, thus enabling Allied battleships to batter Japanese shores in the closing stages of the war. Unlike British carriers, the Essex class did not have armoured flight deck and hangars.

Displacement	27,433 tonnes (27,000 tons)
Length	249·9 m (820 ft)
Beam (extreme)	45 m (147·5 ft)
Draught	6·1 m (20 ft)
Engines	Geared turbines with a shaft power of 111,855 kW (150,000 hp).
Speed	32 knots
Carrier capacity	100 aircraft
Armament	12 127 mm (5 in) guns
	40 40 mm (1·57 in) AA guns
	50 20 mm (0·79 in) guns
Armour	Maximum 76·2 mm (3 in)

in the Pacific were the Japanese I-201 class, able to maintain a remarkable submerged speed of 19 knots for nearly one hour; the Japanese midget submarines and 'human torpedoes'; and, the largest of all non-nuclear submarines, the I-400 class. Designed to launch aircraft against the Panama Canal, they were actually used to carry supplies to Pacific island bases. Some 122 m (400·25 ft) long, and displacing 5791 tonnes (5700 tons), the I-400 had a hangar or cargo hold 31 m (102 ft) long and 3·6 m (12 ft) in diameter.

German U,boats were notably successful in the Battle of the Atlantic during the early years of the war. But by 1943 the convoy system had been perfected, Allied losses fell dramatically, and U-boat losses mounted. Early convoys were protected by a hastily assembled collection of destroyers and corvettes, their crews untrained in escort work and their instruments unable to detect a submarine at a range greater than about 1370 m (1500 yd). Faced with a pack of submarines hunting under cover of darkness, they were relatively helpless, and usually remained unaware of the enemy's presence until actually attacked.

Improvements in the convoy system came in a number of forms. One of the most vital was increased aerial cover, and the improved radar carried by the aircraft. Early CAM (Catapult Equipped Merchant) ships carrying a single fighter aircraft which had to be ditched after one mission, were succeeded by 1942–3 by a fleet of escort carriers. Displacing around 12,192 tonnes (12,000 tons), and operating up to 18 aircraft equipped with radar and depth charges, these craft made it possible to hunt and kill submarines before they attacked the convoy.

Germany's answer was the snorkel—an underwater 'breathing' tube which enabled the U-boats to run their diesel engines and recharge their batteries while submerged. Fortunately for the Allies this provided only a partial solution, for the U-boats of the time had a speed of only 6 knots at snorkel depth. This proved as inadequate for mounting a concerted attack as it was for fleeing from convoy escorts. And as the war progressed these escorts improved in numbers, tactical experience, training and armament.

In face of this opposition Germany developed a new generation of submarines with vastly improved underwater performance and endurance, the Type XXI. However these entered service too late to affect the outcome of the war.

Ships of today's navies

The principal weapons of modern naval warfare are the submarine, the guided missile and aircraft. Despite the vulnerability inherent in their size, aircraft carriers seem likely to retain a place in the navy of the future. But they are the last of the large surface warships. The role of other surface ships is no longer to fight one another, or to bombard shore positions.

It is rather to combat missiles, submarines and aircraft, to protect merchant shipping, and to engage in small scale actions. For these duties a range of ships has been evolved from the smaller warships of World War II, the destroyers, corvettes and frigates.

In the post war years the Soviet and American navies laid down cruisers displacing up to 19,300 tonnes (19,000 tons). The most noteworthy was the USS *Long Beach*, the first nuclear powered surface warship. By earlier standards she was small, displacing several thousand tonnes less than the original *Dreadnought*, but she was much larger than the 'big' ships of today. These, variously known as cruisers, superdestroyers or (in America) frigates, include the American California class, displacing 10,000 tonnes (9842 tons) and measuring 181·7 m (596 ft) in length, and the Soviet Kresta II class which displace only 6000 tonnes (5905 tons). The main armament consists of anti-aircraft and anti-submarine missile launchers, and most ships of this type carry a helicopter. This can assist in the job of locating enemy submarines, and its sonar equipment may be linked to the mother ship's fire control data computing equipment for missile guidance. The helicopter also carries homing torpedoes and anti-ship guided missiles.

The helicopter cruiser is in effect a mini aircraft carrier with a flight deck extending up to half the length of the ship. Most displace some 10,000 tonnes (9842 tons) or less and operate nine or ten helicopters, but the Soviet *Moskva* and *Leningrad* are larger, with 30 helicopters and a displacement of 15,000 tonnes (14,763 tons). They are designed for anti-submarine or amphibious operations, and like the smaller helicopter carriers they carry surface to air and anti-submarine missiles and torpedoes.

Destroyers of today displace up to about 5000 tonnes (4921 tons) and are usually powered by gas turbine or combined diesel and gas turbine engines. Their duties include area defence against aircraft, missiles and submarines, escort work and support in landing operations. The British Type 42 guided missile destroyer class is typical. The ships displace 3657 tonnes (3600 tons), measure 127·1 m (417 ft) in length, and carry a crew of 230 men. They are armed with anti-aircraft, anti-missile and anti-ship guided missiles, and their onboard helicopter carries homing torpedoes and guided missiles. Like most destroyers they are packed with all the latest navigational aids and weapons sensor systems, including ADAWS (Action Data Automation for Weapon Systems). This consists of two computers which co-ordinate, sort,

Opposite: The British guided missile destroyer 'Devonshire' under way (top) and firing a missile (right) from the stern missile launcher. The ship mounts two 115 mm (4·53 in) radar controlled fully automatic quick firing guns in bow turrets.

analyse and display all information from the weapon sensors, and control the missile and gun systems. Two gas turbine engines, each having a shaft power of 18,642 kW (25,000 hp), and controllable pitch propellers give high speed and remarkable manoeuvrability—the Type 42 destroyers can stop from full speed in just 366 m (400 yd).

Destroyer escorts or frigates are essentially scaled down destroyers, displacing between about 2000 and 4000 tonnes (1968 and 3936 tons). With speeds of up to 40 knots they are designed to outpace nuclear submarines, and they carry a mixed armament similar to that of the destroyer. Still smaller ships include corvettes and other fast patrol boats displacing from as little as 90 tonnes (91·4 tons) up to around 1200 tonnes (1181 tons). Designed for patrol, escort or submarine hunting duties in coastal or short radius sea operations and armed with torpedoes, guns or

missiles, their maximum speed is usually in the 40–50 knot range.

Among the small fast patrol and gun boats being developed by advanced navies are two new types of craft, the hydrofoil and hovercraft. The hull of a hydrofoil craft 'flies' above the waves on underwater 'wings' called hydrofoils. Naval types have three fully submerged foils, computer controlled to adjust the angle of each foil to compensate for oncoming waves. These small craft thus provide an exceptionally stable gun platform, and they are remarkably manoeuvrable, being able to stop in roughly twice their length. Speeds of over 40 knots are usual, and one experimental hydrofoil reached 80 knots, so craft of this type may be the fast escort ships of the future.

Hovercraft or surface effect ships ride on a cushion of air and are still faster. The US Navy's experimental SES-100 B, a 23·7 m (78 ft) long 100 tonne (98·4 ton)

hovercraft has attained 82·3 knots. Capable of operating over land and sea, and over swamp and other previously impossible types of terrain, hovercraft have already proved their value in landing operations and in combat.

Following their extensive experience of amphibious assaults in the Pacific during World War II, the US Navy has in recent years pioneered and evolved a new generation of craft for use in amphibious operations. The tank landing ship or LST (landing ship tank) of World War II has been developed into larger, faster and more technically advanced ships such as the USS *Newport* of 1969. Displacing some 8342 tonnes (8210 tons) at full load, *Newport* carries up to 500 troops and a wide range of tanks, trucks and amphibious combat and transport vehicles. In place of the hinged bow and short ramp of earlier types, *Newport* has a 34 m (111·5 ft) hydraulically operated ramp which

is rapidly extended into position by derricks projecting over the bow. While troops and wheeled vehicles land over the ramp, amphibious vehicles travel straight from the hold into the water through stern gates.

In addition the US Navy has helicopter cruisers, commando carriers and amphibious command ships. The latter are designed to act as command centres for combined land, sea, air and amphibious assaults. Finally there is a new type of amphibious assault ship which combines the roles of the LST, the helicopter cruiser and the commando carrier. Displacing around 40,642 tonnes (40,000 tons) it can land a complete assault team and its vehicles by helicopter and landing

Left: A conventional aircraft carrier, the French 'Clemenceau'. Completed in 1961, she carries 40 aircraft, displaces 27,307 tonnes (26,876 tons), is 265 m (869 ft) long, and has a service speed of 24 knots.
Above: A conventional Soviet built Egyptian submarine of the W class.

craft (the latter are carried in a 'dock well' below the flight deck). During an assault operation, the ship's complement of VTOL (vertical takeoff and landing) and STOL (short takeoff and landing) aircraft provides close air support.

Nuclear submarines and surface ships

Submarines of the pre-nuclear age, and conventional submarines today, are strictly submersibles—surface craft capable of limited underwater operations. Their diesel engines burn oxygen and produce noxious exhaust fumes, and can only be used when surfaced or at snorkel depth. For submerged operations they rely on battery driven electric motors. Submerged speed and range are thus severely limited by the fact that the craft must surface to recharge batteries at frequent intervals. Even the most advanced conventional submarines can only cruise underwater for a maximum of four days at low speed, or an hour or two at high speed.

During World War II the German scientist Hellmuth Walther invented a turbine engine independent of outside air. In it, hydrogen peroxide was broken down to produce oygen and water. The oxygen was ignited with diesel fuel, and the heat produced was used to generate steam for the turbines. This represented a significant improvement. But the true submarine, capable of virtually unlimited underwater operations, had to await the advent of nuclear power. The possibilities were appreciated before World War II, and development began at the US Naval Research Laboratory in Washington DC in 1939. However it was brought to a halt when nuclear research was diverted to producing an atomic bomb, and was not resumed until after the war.

The first nuclear powered submarine, *Nautilus*, was completed in 1955. Her top speed was around 20 knots, surfaced or submerged, while her range on her first fuel core was 100,681 km (62,582 miles). Equipped with generators and distillers to produce oxygen (for breathing) and fresh water from the sea, she could remain submerged for months at a time. In 1960 the later US submarine *Triton* circumnavigated the globe underwater, steaming 66,788 km (41,500 miles) in 83 days.

The nuclear power plant of an atomic ship replaces the traditional boiler, and consists basically of a nuclear fission reactor. This generates enormous quantities of heat from a very small amount of fuel. The speed of the reaction, and hence the quantity of heat generated, is adjusted by raising or lowering control rods into the reactor core. The heat is used to produce steam which in turn drives the ship's turbine engines. These normally turn the propeller through reduction gears, but on some submarines the turbine generates electricity to power electric motors.

Nautilus and her immediate successors were traditional in shape, but nuclear power was soon applied to a new generation of submarines with the hull form pioneered by the conventionally powered *Albacore*. The rounded bow and tapering teardrop shaped hull—which is free from all protuberances except for the 'sail' tower and the control surfaces—gave higher speeds and much improved manoeuvrability, and led *Albacore's* officers to coin the word 'hydrobatics'. The Skipjack, Thresher and Sturgeon classes of American nuclear submarines all have teardrop hulls, as does the Los Angeles class of which the first four were commissioned in 1975-6. These, the fastest of all submarines, are believed to have a submerged speed in the region of 45 knots.

Armed either with tactical missiles for attacks on

Above: A Polaris missile fired from the submerged submarine HMS 'Revenge'.
Right: An American Polaris submarine, the 'Abraham Lincoln'.

hostile submarines or surface ships, or with strategic missiles, the nuclear submarines of today's navies can and do roam the oceans of the world at unprecedented depths where they are virtually undetectable. They are also out of reach of all conventional methods of communication and navigation. Surfacing at frequent intervals to make use of radio or celestial navigation systems would of course negate the point of the nuclear submarine. Instead a computerised version of one of the oldest of all navigational aids—dead reckoning—has been evolved. Dead (the word is a contraction of 'deduced') reckoning involves estimating speed and direction and from this deducing one's position relative to a known starting point. In the past it was more a matter of instinct and inspired guesswork than a science. But the nuclear submarine's inertial guidance system produces errors in the region of only 1 km (0·61 miles) after a week's continuous cruising. It relies on a combination of gyroscopes, accelerometers (devices which detect and measure acceleration) and computer. Three gyroscopes are set up in three planes at right angles to each other, to provide a steady frame of reference. Accelerometers coupled to each in the same three planes are sensitive enough to detect the smallest deviation from this frame of reference. Their measurements are fed into a computer which can either plot the submarine's course from a known starting point or can be programmed with the desired course, in which case it acts as an automatic pilot.

Although the greatest benefits of nuclear power are reaped by submarines, this type of propulsion is also used to advantage in increasing numbers of surface warships. The virtually unlimited cruising range is the most obvious reward. The US carrier *Enterprise* steamed over 321,870 km (200,000 miles) before her first refuelling, and the most recent nuclear ships can cover twice that distance. Sustained high speed is another virtue. The nuclear cruiser *Long Beach*, and destroyers such as *Bainbridge* and *Truxtun* can maintain almost indefinitely a top speed which probably exceeds 35 knots. In addition the absence of massive boilers and fuel bunkers frees valuable space for weapons systems, stores and so on. The advantages are thus great enough to outweigh the increased expense, and as nuclear power plants become more compact and less costly they will be installed in a greater variety and number of surface warships.

Merchant ships in the machine age

The birth of the steamship

The first steam engines, designed for pumping water from mines, were large, inefficient and single acting—with a 'push' stroke but no 'pull' to follow it. All early attempts at using them to drive boats failed, and in at least one case the boat sank under the excessive weight.

The first to succeed in moving against a current was the French Marquis Claude de Jouffroy's *Pyroscaphe* of 1783. It steamed briefly and hesitantly up the River Saône, France, propelled by side paddle wheels which the piston turned through a ratchet mechanism.

In America James Rumsey produced a steamboat

with water jet propulsion, and John Fitch built a curious craft propelled by 12 oar like paddles suspended vertically along the sides. In 1790 his improved model, *Experiment*, inaugurated the world's first regular steamboat service. Running between Philadelphia and Trenton on the Delaware river, *Experiment* was driven by three paddles at the stern and attained a speed of almost seven knots. The route was, however, well served by stage coach, and lack of profits forced Fitch to abandon his project.

By this time the steam engine had been radically improved by James Watt, and in 1801 the Scottish engineer William Symington built a sturdy steam tug, *Charlotte Dundas*. Fitted with a stern paddle wheel, this 17 m (56 ft) craft towed barges along the Forth-Clyde canal until she was forcibly retired after complaints that her wash was eroding the canal banks. The steamboat had arrived, but nobody seemed to want it.

Undeterred by the apparent unpopularity of steam power, and by his own failure to impress the emperor Napoleon with a steam powered invasion barge, the American inventor Robert Fulton went on to build his famous *North River Steamboat of Clermont*. With this 40·5 m (133 ft) paddle steamer Fulton operated the first commercially successful steamer service in 1807. *Clermont* plied back and forth between New York and Albany, and a contemporary observer wrote: 'The velocity of the steamboat is calculated at four miles an hour (3·5 knots). It is said it will make a progress of two against the current of the Mississippi, and if so it will certainly be a very valuable acquisition to the commerce of our western states.' He was right. The legendary Mississippi paddle steamers became a symbol of the recklessness and glamour of pioneering life in the deep south.

Commercial steamboat services followed on Euro-

Below: Brunel's 'Great Britain' on her maiden voyage across the Atlantic.

Above, top: 'Stockholmshaxan' (Witch of Stockholm), an early propeller driven steamboat built in 1816. Above, centre: Brunel's third ship, the leviathan 'Great Eastern' of 1859. Designed to carry 4000 passengers on the Australian run, and the only ship with paddles, screw and sails, she was 207 m (680 ft) long. A commercial failure as a passenger ship, she spent her short working life as a cable layer. Above, bottom: 'Robert F. Stockton', 1838, the first iron hulled ship to cross the Atlantic (under sail), and the first merchant ship with screw propulsion.

Above: 'Thomas Anderson', 1889, an early steel hulled ship with screw propulsion.

pean inland waters, led by Henry Bell's *Comet* of 1812. But the steamboat had yet to venture out to sea.

Steam across the Atlantic

Many years passed before the public agreed to risk an ocean voyage under steam. In 1819 the American captain Moses Rogers equipped a sailing packet with steam power and elegant passenger accommodation. But despite financial backing and much advertising

his ship, *Savannah*, made her first Atlantic crossing with neither passengers nor cargo. Rogers continued on a publicity voyage to Sweden and Russia, but was eventually forced to remove *Savannah's* engine and sell her as a sailing ship. Widely misrepresented as the first steamship to cross the Atlantic, *Savannah* was in reality a sailing ship with a small auxiliary engine with a shaft power of 56 kW (75 hp), and her so-called 'epic' voyage was almost entirely powered by sail.

However her voyage inspired journalists to enthusiastic eulogies, aroused the general public's interest, and stimulated engineers and shipbuilders to forge ahead. Steam ferries began plying on short sea crossings from England to France and Ireland. And when in 1835 the celebrated British engineer Isambard Kingdom Brunel suggested that Britain's Great Western Railway should be extended across the Atlantic with a steamboat service from Bristol to New York, his idea was accepted.

Brunel's ship, the *Great Western*, was laid down in 1836 and launched in the following year. After fitting out, she set sail on her maiden voyage to New York on 8 April 1838. Onlookers marvelled at her 'magnificent proportions and stupendous machinery'. The British and American Steam Navigation Company, a rival in the race to be first across the Atlantic, had already chartered and dispatched the Irish packet *Sirius*, which sailed from Cork, Ireland on 4 April. *Sirius* beat *Great Western* by just four hours after a voyage under continuous steam power that lasted 18 days and 10 hours, and received a hero's welcome. 'It was', in the words of one of *Great Western*'s passengers, 'an exciting moment—a moment of triumph! Experiment then ceased—certainty was attained.' *Great Western* had of course made a much faster crossing. The first steamship designed for the Atlantic run, she was 71·9 m (236 ft) long and 10·7 m (35 ft) in the beam.

The liner era
Both *Sirius* and *Great Western* carried a full complement of masts and sails, both were paddle steamers, and both were wooden. They differed in little more than size and detail from Fulton's *Clermont*. Compared to them Brunel's next ship, *Great Britain*, was a revelation. Launched in 1843 she was the first iron hulled ocean going ship, the first with screw propulsion, and the first propeller driven ship to cross the Atlantic. Dwarfing all predecessors, she measured 88 m (289 ft) in length, had cabins for 360 passengers, and averaged 9·3 knots on the Atlantic run. Described once as the 'forefather of all modern ships', *Great Britain* marked the beginning of the liner era. For a little over a century shipping companies such as Cunard and the Collins Line vied with each other for the honour of the Blue Riband—the title given to the liner providing the fastest Atlantic crossing.

Ships grew steadily faster and more luxurious. In 1889 the second *City of Paris*, the first of a new generation of steel hulled twin screw liners, became the first to make the crossing in under six days, at an average of 20 knots. In 1909 the Cunarder *Mauretania*, perhaps the most famous of them all, pushed the speed up to 26·06 knots. The first turbine engined liner, she held the Blue Riband for over 20 years until it was won in turn by *Bremen* (1929, 28 knots), *Normandie* (1935, 31·3 knots), and *Queen Mary* (1938, 31·69 knots).

The race culminated in 1952 when the *United States* crossed the Atlantic in three and a half days at an average of 35·59 knots (her top speed was 41·75 knots). She was 301·8 m (990 ft) long and 30·97 m (101·6 ft) in the beam, and carried over 2000 passengers and a crew of 1093. But she had arrived too late. For 15 years or so she, and others such as *France* and the Cunard *Queens*, plied the oceans with ever fewer passengers until economic necessity forced them to retire. Their race, and their role as ferryboats, had been lost to the jet airliner. A few continue in service as floating hotels and holiday cruise ships, but with the exception of Cunard's *QE2* none can compare in size and splendour with the great ships of the golden age of the Atlantic ferry.

Left: The 'Great Republic' of 1886, owned by the Pacific Mail Steam-Ship Company and designed for the trans-Pacific mail service. Built over 40 years after the all iron screw propelled 'Great Britain', she was—with her wooden hull, paddle propulsion and primitive 'walking beam' engine—remarkably outdated in design and construction.

Below: Two Mississippi stern wheeler paddle steamers. the 'Mississippi' (top) and the 'Delta Queen' (bottom). Caustically described as 'wheel barrows' by captains of the earlier side wheelers, the stern wheelers were cheaper to run. Races between these 'showboats' of the Mississippi and Missouri created a fever of excitement and were accompanied by extravagant bets and considerable danger.

Above: The Cunard 'Queen Elizabeth II'. Launched in 1967 she is the world's sole remaining large luxury liner. Equipped as a cruise ship, she is 293·5 m (963 ft) long, carries over 2000 passengers, and cruises at 28·5 knots.

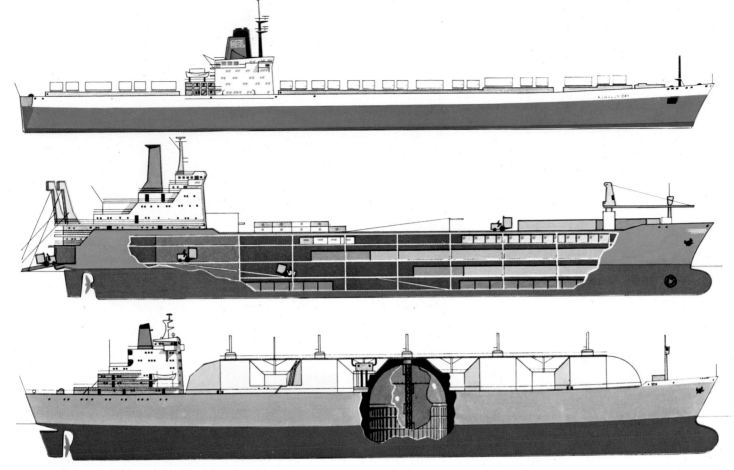

Left, and above top: Container ships. The photograph shows clearly how the hold is divided into container sized 'cells', while the drawing shows how the containers are also stacked on the deck above the holds. Loading and discharge take place simultaneously, the sequence of operations having been previously worked out by computer. By prepacking miscellaneous and widely varied cargoes, containerization brings the benefits of the bulk carrier to the transport of general cargo. Rapid turn round reduces the time spent in port from around 75 per cent of the ship's working life for general cargo ships to some 20 per cent, and transport and packing costs can be as much as 50 per cent lower than usual.
Above, centre: Roll on/roll off provides a further method of speeding loading and discharge.
Above: A specialized bulk carrier for liquid natural gas, which is transported at a temperature of −161°C, hence the protective 'domes'.

Cargo ships today

Forty or fifty years ago the passenger liners were the giants among merchantmen. Today that role has passed to the more utilitarian oil tanker. And it is perhaps a sign of the times that tankers are large solely because the bigger a bulk ship is the cheaper it is to operate—whereas the liners were giants partly because people enjoyed and were prepared to pay for their grandeur and splendour. However, though lacking in the beauty traditionally associated with ships, the VLCCs (Very Large Crude Carriers) are impressive feats of engineering and technology. The French built Batilus, the largest at the time of writing (1977), is 400 m (1312 ft) long, 63 m (206·6 ft) in the beam, has a draught of 28·5 m (93·5 ft), and is of 551,100 tonnes (542,400 tons) deadweight—this is a measure of cargo capacity. Still larger VLCCs have been planned, including an articulated million tonne monster hinged amidships to ride more easily over the waves. But with the energy crisis of the mid-1970s and tens of millions of tonnes of tankers already laid up, Batilus may remain the largest ship ever built for a long time.

General cargo ships which load and discharge a wide variety of goods at a series of ports en route remain an essential part of all merchant fleets. But the emphasis today is on specialized ships which can be turned round rapidly and therefore waste little time in port. These range from tankers, container and other bulk ships, to the recent LASH (Lighter Aboard SHip) and SeaBee vessels. In both of these cases, cargo is packed in lighters—massive floating containers—which are then floated out and taken on board by special lifting gear built into the ship. Loading and discharge are quick, and ships of this type need no dock.

With the notable exception of supertankers which are usually powered by steam turbines, almost all modern cargo ships have diesel engines. America, Germany and Japan have experimented with nuclear powered merchant ships, but despite their technical success these have proved economically unviable. However, nuclear propulsion plants will probably become smaller and cheaper, and this combined with ever rising fuel prices may lead to the widespread adoption of nuclear power for large merchantmen.

Explorers of yesterday and today

Setting off into the unknown, whether to new markets for trade or simply out of curiosity, seafarers have more than any other group opened up the world. This was never more true than in the late 15th and early 16th centuries, when Europe sought new routes to the riches of the Orient. Prince Henry of Portugal—Henry the Navigator—made himself the focus of the search for a route around Africa, setting up what amounted to a research institute concerned with everything to do with ships, the sea, navigation and chart making. To his 'school' came experts, enthusiasts and adventurers from all over Europe.

Henry's groundwork prepared the way for Bartolomeo Diaz' historic voyage of 1487–8. Diaz set sail from Lisbon with two small caravels and a third supply ship, and at first everything went smoothly as they sailed southwards down Africa's west coast. The initial legs of the journey were by then familiar territory, but off Walfish Bay, South West Africa, strong winds drove Diaz' ships out of sight of land. The wind soon turned to a northerly gale, and there was nothing to be done but let the gale drive them on southwards. After an anxious 13 days the storm abated. Diaz assumed that he had been carried south parallel to the African coast, to which there was no known end, and he headed east. Several days passed with no sight of land, the crew's anguish growing with each succeeding day as they were, it seemed, lost for ever in unknown seas.

Fortunately, justifying his worth as a true explorer, Diaz had an inspiration—perhaps they had rounded the unknown southern tip of Africa. He accordingly altered course to the north, and soon sighted land, sailing in to anchor at what is now Mossel Bay, South Africa. His crew were unwilling to risk their lives again, so after a brief exploration of the southern tip of Africa the expedition turned for home. It was left to Vasco da Gama to complete the voyage to India in 1497–8.

Left: A detail from 'Portuguese carracks off a rocky coast', by Anthoniszoon, 1521. The ships of Columbus, Magellan and Vespucci were of the same type.

The New World

Diaz had succeeded by virtue of his open mind. The achievements of the most famous of all the explorers of the great age of discovery, Christopher Columbus, were dimmed by a mind unable to break away from its own preconceptions. Columbus expected to reach the Orient after a passage of some 4,100 km (2,550 miles) to the west. He had first asked Portugal to sponsor his expedition, but the Portuguese dismissed him as a 'vainglorious babbler'. However, after several strenuous attempts and much confused theorising, he finally persuaded the Spaniards to help him, and his three ships departed on 3 August 1492. They reached the Canaries on 12 August, setting sail again on 6 September, travelling boldy west into totally unknown regions.

Now Columbus' true qualities as an adventurer and a leader emerged. His faith in his 'mission' overcame the doubts and fears of his men, who were for the most part sceptical about the whole venture, and it enabled him to pass lightly over the erratic behaviour of his compass (this was due to the then unknown phenomenon of magnetic variation).

On 12 October, 36 days out from the Canaries, the expedition thankfully sighted land and Columbus went ashore to plant the Spanish flag. The land, named San Salvador by Columbus, was in the Bahama Islands, but here Columbus the 'babbler' took over again. Convinced that he had reached 'the islands which are set down in maps at the end of the Orient', he decided to sail on to see whether 'I can come across the Island of Cipango' (Japan). This he identified in Cuba.

Nothing that he found could shake his conviction, and he returned to Spain to a magnificent reception and a shower of honours and priviledges. Three further voyages left him as sure as ever, but by then he had made many enemies, and a rival explorer had appeared on the scene—Amerigo Vespucci. Previously engaged in the business of outfitting ships, he had met Columbus before the latter's third voyage. He obtained first Spanish and then Portuguese support for a series of westward expeditions between

Above: A modern reconstruction of the galleon 'Golden Hind' in which Sir Francis Drake sailed around the world (1577–81). Details and even dimensions of the 31 m (102 ft) replica were based mainly on conjecture. Drake set out on his voyage with one aim: to harass the Spanish and challenge their supremacy in central and southern America. He achieved notable success, but in the end was forced to flee westwards thus circumnavigating the globe by accident.

1497 and 1504. Following at first the now almost routine course pioneered by Columbus, Vespucci went on to explore the coastline of the south American continent. He sailed south, probably discovering the mouth of the Amazon. And he made a number of astronomical calculations. Discounting the ancient Latin astronomer Ptolemy's estimate of 33,330 km

Above: A modern reconstruction of the Pilgrim Fathers' ship 'Mayflower', 1620.

(20,710 miles) and Columbus' lower figure, Vespucci calculated the circumference of the earth at around 39,995 km (24,852 miles). This must have instilled doubt as to whether the lands discovered by Columbus and himself were indeed part of Asia. And when on his voyage of 1501–2 he sailed down the coast of south America to the River Plate and beyond, the light suddenly dawned. He returned to Portugal and announced:

> There is much more to this earth than Europe and Asia and Africa. There is also a New World, a new half of the earth, a never before dreamed of Western Hemisphere. There is a whole new continent waiting for the men of Europe to explore and possess and thereon to begin a new civilization.

It now remained for Ferdinand Magellan to discover a way through this new world to Asia, and for the Pilgrim Fathers to begin 'a new civilization' in the country which took its name from Amerigo Vespucci—America. Magellan, a Portuguese nobleman by birth, spent his early career as a naval seaman helping his country in its successful attempt to break Muslim power in the Indian Ocean, thereby completing the task begun by Diaz of opening trade with the East to Portuguese ships. Then, after a rebuff by the king of Portugal, Magellan transferred his allegiance to Spain, for whom he proposed to seek out the alternative route to the wealth of the orient through or around America.

His expedition of five ships and 234 men set out on 20 September 1519, with provisions to last for two years. When his first hope, the estuary of the River Plate, proved illusory, he continued south. After quelling a mutiny, losing one ship on a shoal, and fighting his way south through storms and bitter cold, he at last found a passage, and on 'Wednesday, 28th November, 1520, we debouched from that strait engulfing ourselves in the Pacific Sea'. Magellan's discovery of the straits named after him would have sufficed for most people, but he was determined to continue westward across the Pacific to the Spice Islands (Moluccas). He himself was killed in the Philippines, but the remainder of his expedition sailed on. On 6 September 1522 the survivors—just 18 men and one ship—returned to Spain, having completed the first circumnavigation of the world.

While Magellan had been cursed by a dishonest chandler, who had supplied only half the quantity of provisions agreed, the Pilgrim Fathers suffered one unseaworthy ship (the *Speedwell*), and fierce storms. Pilgrims and supplies from *Speedwell* were taken onto

the group's other ship, *Mayflower*, which set sail across the Atlantic on 6 September 1620. *Mayflower* was a three masted square rigged ship probably about 27·5 m (90 ft) in length. A replica, as much the fruit of inspired guesswork as of factual knowledge, was built and sailed from England to Massachusetts, America, in 1957. The voyage took 53 days, compared to the original Mayflower's 66 days. The Pilgrim Fathers had been granted the territory of Virginia, but stormy seas forced them to land first at Provincetown and finally at the site of Plymouth, Massachusetts, there founding the first permanent New England colony.

Charting the world

After the voyages of discovery of Diaz, da Gama, Columbus and Magellan, maps of the world took on an almost modern appearance. However, three large regions still lay wide open for exploration. These were the 'northwest passage' believed to exist around the top of America; the 'northeast passage' to the north of Scandinavia and Russia; and the dream of an unknown continent in the Pacific, the *Terra Incognita Australis*. Famous explorers such as John and Sebastian Cabot, Martin Frobisher and William Barents devoted their energies to the first two. Success did not materialize until much later, with voyages by, for example, Fridtjof Nansen (whose ship *Fram* drifted in the ice from the New Siberian Islands to Spitzbergen, 1893–6), and by the American nuclear submarines *Nautilus* and *Skate* which cruised beneath the ice cap in 1958.

Australasia was pursued in turn by Abel Tasman, William Dampier and Captain James Cook. After a spell surveying the coasts of Newfoundland for the British navy, Cook was sent out to chart the islands of the Pacific and to determine the extent of Australia —and to claim it for Britain. An experienced explorer

Above: Cook's 'Resolution' in Antarctica.
Right: 'Galway Blazer', the unconventional junk-rigged boat in which Commander W. King attempted a single handed non stop 0 circumnavigation.
Pages 100-101: 'Gipsy Moth IV', the yacht in which Sir Francis Chichester sailed around the world in 1966–7. His voyage included a 24,972 km (15,517 mile) 119 day stretch (from Sydney, Australia, to Plymouth, England) made without a single port of call.
Pages 102-3: 'Suhaili' the 9·75 m (32 ft) ketch in which Robin Knox-Johnston won the 1968 'Sunday Times' (London) award for the first person to sail single handed non stop around the world.

and seaman, Cook chose his ship carefully:

A ship of this kind must not be of a great draught of water, yet of a sufficient burden and capacity to carry a proper quantity of provisions and necessaries for her complement of men, and for the term requisite to perform the voyage. She must also be of a construction that will bear to take the ground and of a size which, in case of necessity, may be safely and conveniently laid on shore to repair any accidental damage or defect. These properties are not to be found in ships of war of forty guns, nor in frigates, nor in East India Company's ships, nor in large three-decked West India ships, nor indeed in any other but North-country ships such as are built for the coal trade, which are peculiarly adapted for this purpose.

The success of Cook's voyages of 1768–71 demonstrated the wisdom of his choice of the Whitby collier.

Today the oceans of the world have all been thoroughly charted, and ships depend more on technology than on the seafarer's art, instinct and spirit of adventure. In modern times the only exploits comparable to those of the past are those of the lone yachtsmen—some of whose boats are illustrated on the last pages of this book—and of scientific explorers such as Thor Heyerdahl, who crossed the Pacific and Atlantic respectively in his balsa and papyrus craft *Kon Tiki* and *Ra*.

Index

Page numbers in italics refer to illustration captions.

ACKNOWLEDGEMENTS

The publishers would like to thank the following organisations and individuals for their kind permission to reproduce the photographs in this book:

Reproduced by Gracious Permission of Her Majesty the Queen 18–19; Jean-Pierre Anazel (Musée de la Marine Paris) 38, 45; Bapty 70–71; Barnaby's Picture Library 12; Beken of Cowes 49, 96, 97; Bodleian Library, Oxford 15; Camera Press 47 right, 83, (J. Messerschmidt) 60 right, 61; Camera & Pen International 100–101; Cassell & Company Limited 102; "The Connoisseur" 20–21; Crown Copyright 74–75, 77 above and below; Mike Davis 44, 86 right, 87; Greene Line Steamers 89; Michael Holford 40 below, 42–43, 52 below, (National Maritime Museum) 55, 88, 98; Robert Hunt Library 58–59; Jacqueline Hyde 28, 29; Douglas Lobley 90–91; Mariners Museum, Newport News 40 above; Merseyside County Museum, Department of Maritime History ends; Ministry of Defence title (Royal Navy) 82; National Maritime Museum 22, 24–25, 31, 41, 66, 84–85, (Cooper-Bridgeman) 26, (Robert Hunt Library) 32 above, 32 below, 33 below, 36–37; Octopus Books 8, 13, 86 left; Palazzo Ducale, Venice 16–17; Parker Gallery 52 above, 54, 99; Picturepoint contents, 6, 7; Popperfoto 9, 62–63 left; P&O Line 46–47 left; Scala 23; Spectrum Colour Library 78–79, 81 above; Universitet i Bergen Historisk Museum, Norway 39; Universitetets Oldsaksamling, Oslo 14; Derek Witty 34–35, 94; Zefa 92.